Italian Cooking Like Nonna

➤❖❮

Italian Cooking Like Nonna

>*<

Authentic Family Recipes with
Extraordinary Flavor and Endless Variations

Caroline De Luca

Creator of The Delightful Cook

PAGE STREET
PUBLISHING CO.

PAGE STREET
PUBLISHING CO.

First published in 2021 by
Page Street Publishing Co.
27 Congress Street, Suite 105
Salem, MA 01970
www.pagestreetpublishing.com

Distributed by Macmillan, sales in Canada by The Canadian Manda Group.

25 24 23 22 21   1 2 3 4 5

ISBN-13: 978-1-64567-392-7
ISBN-10: 1-64567-392-8

Library of Congress Control Number: 2021931388

Cover and book design by Page Street Publishing Co.
Photography by Caroline De Luca

Printed and bound in the United States

Dedication

❯❮

For all the dreamers.

Sommario ←

Introduction

Simplicity is the only word that comes to mind when talking about Italian cooking. Since many dishes comprise so few ingredients, the fundamentals of authentic Italian home cooking are based on the use of excellent-quality ingredients. With the elimination of all artificial items and processed foods, home cooks depend heavily on lean meats, seafood, fresh fruit, dairy products, vegetables and, of course, good-quality olive oil.

After the fall of the Roman Empire, the different Italian cities began to form their own customs and traditions. The regions began adapting their cooking methods to develop new and exciting techniques and variations, some of which have continued to this day. *Cucina povera,* which translates to "poor cooking," is a philosophy that is very popular in Italian cooking, as it is in many other cuisines worldwide. Fresh seasonal produce is used to create humble dishes that bring families together. It is a tradition that has been used and followed by many Italian families, whether they live in Italy or another country.

Back in the old country, my grandparents lived off what the land produced for them. The fresh vegetables and fruits they grew were the main ingredients readily available to them. As meat and fish were deemed quite expensive at that time, they were used only on special occasions. Every part of the animal would be used when cooking, leaving nothing to waste. They took it upon themselves to work with what they had, experimented with many flavor combinations and turned them into some stunning meals, which we still continue to make to this day. My grandparents both came from large families, and while growing up they had the responsibilities of doing the daily chores—including cooking for the whole family. With very little money, they didn't have access to the luxuries that we are so blessed with today. What they did have was an intuitive way to create authentic, wholesome food, illustrating what their country had to offer.

My food journey started at the tender age of seven. I grew up in a big Italian family, and it was definitely no secret that we all shared a love for food. I would spend hours on end in the kitchen watching my family create fabulous recipes with pure joy. What struck me the most was how well they would use their creativity and intuition when it came to making a simple meal. They seemed to have a unique flair for making a meal without looking at a piece of paper, then this magnificent dish would appear out of nowhere and be displayed proudly on the table for all to enjoy.

Twenty-eight years later, it fascinates me to see my eighty-five-year-old nonna still practice this way of cooking every time she sets foot in the kitchen, producing gorgeous dishes from pure knowledge and heart. I don't think my nonna has ever picked up a cookbook! She watches her Italian cooking shows, picks up on little hints and tricks and tries them out in the kitchen. That's fascinating in itself and an approach that I wanted to explore even more. Sure, cookbooks are amazing in their own right, but how many of us start a recipe and then soon veer off course? We sometimes add alternative ingredients or want to use up what we have left over in the fridge to prevent waste. I don't know about you, but I hate to see any type of food go to waste. Perhaps using what we have is all that we need to create the next masterpiece in the kitchen!

I steered away from cooking in my late teens and early twenties, as I was preoccupied with life at the time. It was not until I hit thirty that I found a new appreciation for authentic home cooking, and when I moved out of my home to live on my own, I adopted this method of cooking. I would use simple staple ingredients, which I could alter and adapt to suit my style of cooking. I soon began to realize I was using techniques and methods that followed the old traditions I had seen when I was a child. It was like they had been imprinted in my mind, they flowed so naturally.

This was the moment I created my business and food blog, The Delightful Cook. Without any formal culinary training, I found myself sharing my meals through my social media pages, first with my family and friends and soon, the world. For someone who thrives on creativity, I found this form of expression very rewarding, fulfilling and authentic. From there, I began to explore with even more depth and detail, teaching myself how to write recipes and use a camera, expanding my knowledge in these respective fields and experimenting more in the kitchen. I then took a trip to Italy, which gave me so much more insight into rustic and authentic home cooking and how Italians still used these simple methods. After being totally immersed in the culture and history of the motherland and, of course, food, I came back to Australia implementing these methods into my everyday cooking—sticking to the simplicity of good-quality seasonal ingredients that could be adapted at any time.

The Italian people care very deeply about their family's traditions and customs, especially their cooking traditions, which have been passed down from generation to generation. Most families have signature recipes that have been passed down, and I've shared some of my family's recipes in this book. You will find extremely simple recipes that have not only been made time and time again, but can also be easily adapted to suit your cooking style. I have always said that you really need only a few ingredients to make an inviting meal, and it is how well you can use your creativity and intuition that really makes a masterpiece.

My Mum's Homemade Sugo di Pomodoro (page 14) is an authentic pasta sauce featured in many recipes throughout these chapters, including Rotolo di Spinaci (page 48), Beef Braciole (page 102) and Involtini di Melanzane (page 136), to name a few. It is the perfect sauce base that can be adapted to your own creative way of cooking and turned into a Bolognese Sauce (page 16) or Vegetarian Sauce (page 18). Italians love to make homemade pasta and pizza, and I go through the basic steps for making homemade pizza dough (page 38), orecchiette pasta (page 28) and fettuccine pasta (page 35), which can be used with any of the delicious sauces in the Pasta Perfetto chapter (page 45).

This book will not only help and guide you to become more in tune with your own capabilities but also give you the freedom to really get creative in the kitchen and develop your own cooking style. It will give you the confidence to trust yourself and your instincts so you can cook without a book.

I believe if you can absolutely master the basics when it comes to Italian home cooking, then the world is your oyster. When cooking a recipe I enjoy, I tend to make it several times, ensuring I get the basic elements right to begin with. After I have made it more than twice, I take my own path to create my own version. This is how this book is designed to be used. Start with the base recipe, which can easily be ingrained into your thought process. Then, as time passes, you'll start to feel more comfortable adding or removing ingredients every time you get inspiration in the kitchen. The variation and substitution ideas listed in the recipe introductions are to give you an encouraging guide, helping you expand your creativity and to cook more intuitively. Try different flavors, pair unusual ingredients together—which may not work judging from appearances but, when paired, create enticing flavors.

Remember, even the greatest chefs were once home cooks. They started with basics and learned over time, while practicing techniques to create depth of flavor, and thus discovered what worked in their favor. You do not need to be of Italian blood to cook like an Italian. All you really need is to be willing to try anything new, lots of heart and, of course, passion.

Caroline
x

Chapter One

The Complete Italian Essentials

There is something so very therapeutic about making something by hand. For a few hours it takes you away, and you're completely focused on what you are creating. Growing up, everything was home-made, whether it be a sweet dessert, pasta or pizza. This is the family tradition I have followed throughout the years and still continue to this very day.

When you grow up in an Italian household, knowing basic cooking essentials is expected. Obviously, the different techniques require some practice and time to learn, but they are embedded in us at a very young age. We are shown how to mix flour, eggs and water together, kneading the dough to make homemade tagliatelle, or how to keep a close eye on the yeast to see when it is proved enough to be able to add it to the flour when making bread. I was lucky enough to be surrounded by people in my family who loved to cook. I would study their techniques and learn how to make them my own.

No Italian kitchen would be complete without the fundamentals, and in this chapter I take you on a journey to show you how you can make your own homemade delights that can include the whole family. I believe every good Italian pasta or pizza dish starts with a magnificent sauce, which is why I have included my Mum's Homemade Sugo di Pomodoro (page 14). This is not only a delicious sauce, but it also allows you to freely alter and adapt according to your palate, including a meaty, rich Bolognese Sauce (page 16) and a Vegetarian Sauce (page 18).

Pasta is another standout homemade essential, and in this chapter you can experiment with the different techniques to make traditional homemade pasta, which then can be used in one of the many recipes in my Pasta Perfetto chapter (page 45). Try my Fettuccine Puttanesca (page 60) with home-made fettuccine using the guide on page 35 or homemade cavatelli with semolina flour on page 30.

Learning these simple techniques has helped me become a better cook and appreciate how much love and passion goes into it all. Once you learn the art of making the basics, they will become part of you.

Mum's Homemade Sugo di Pomodoro

Sugo di pomodoro ("tomato sauce") is a staple in any Italian household and is the base of Italian cooking. The beauty of this recipe is that it is extremely versatile and can be used in many other Italian dishes. Toward the end of summer, my entire family would get together on a Saturday morning for a busy day ahead, to create a year's worth of sauce. These jars would be given to the family by the case to be used in many dishes all year.

My brother and I, being the only children at the time, would help out any way we could—whether it was feeding the fresh tomatoes through the tomato milling machine or filling up many empty beer bottles of fresh product. At the end of the day, we would be covered head to toe in tomatoes, enjoying every moment and never wanting it to end. It is a childhood memory that will be with me forever.

Italian mothers all have a signature dish that they cook religiously. From chicken cutlets and baked fish to pasta or meatballs, there is always one thing they cook really well. In my mum's case it is sugo di pomodoro. I remember walking into the kitchen while it was simmering on the stove, thinking it was the best thing in the world, and it was! There is nothing like the taste of fresh homemade pasta sauce spread all over crusty ciabatta.

Of course, we tend to go a little overboard on quantities, but it is all for a very good reason. You never know when an emergency container of sauce will be needed at any given time. When we make large batches of this sauce, we divide it into smaller containers and freeze it, so it can be added to other dishes.

I've spoken to so many people, and they each have their own signature tomato sauce recipe. From fresh or canned tomatoes to adding anchovies or beef bones, they have created their own singular versions of sauce and have passed them on to the next generation.

There are absolutely no rules when it comes to making this sauce. I've started off with a classic base, which you can experiment with as much as your heart desires. This is absolutely perfect for some of the recipes I have in this cookbook: Involtini di Melanzane (page 136), Rotolo di

Spinaci (page 48), Beef Braciole (page 102) and Classic Margherita Pizza (page 72), just to name a few.

Think about the dish you want to make and ask yourself what ingredients would complement it. Use your imagination; the possibilities are endless! I strongly urge you to be as creative as you can in the kitchen. Building on my mum's signature recipe, I've added some lovely alternatives and additions so you can make your own sugo di pomodoro.

The following recipe makes quite a large batch, so it's perfect for dividing into containers to freeze. The sauce can be kept in the freezer for up to 3 months and can be used for pizzas, pastas, focaccias, meat, fish and seafood dishes. The sauces that follow this (Bolognese [page 16], Vegetarian [page 18] and Hazelnut Pesto [page 20]) are the starting point from which you can adapt your own distinctive flavors that your whole family will enjoy.

→ **Makes 67.6 oz (2 L)** ←

Ingredients

¼ cup (60 ml) extra virgin olive oil

2 or 3 cloves garlic, roughly chopped

1 white onion, finely chopped

2 tbsp (30 g) butter

2 tbsp (30 g) tomato paste

1 (14-oz [400-g]) can diced tomatoes

2 (25-oz [700-g]) bottles passata or 2 (28-oz [800-g]) cans tomato puree

1 or 2 bay leaves

Fresh or dried herbs, such as rosemary, oregano, thyme or basil, to taste

1–2 tsp (2–4 g) dried red pepper flakes (optional)

Salt and freshly ground black pepper

Method

In a large saucepan, heat the olive oil over low heat. Add the garlic and onion, and cook for 2 to 3 minutes, until the onion is translucent. Add the butter and stir until melted. Stir in the tomato paste and cook it for 1 to 2 minutes, until it melts into the butter. Tomato paste is very concentrated, so this method will allow its intense flavor to come out and create a really rich sauce.

Pour in the diced tomatoes and tomato puree, and stir. Fill the cans with a little water, shake and pour the contents into the saucepan. This is an Italian ritual, so nothing goes to waste!

It's time to season the sauce. Add the bay leaves. I like to use a combination of 1 to 2 teaspoons (1 to 2 g) of dried herbs such as rosemary or oregano to create a woody, peppery flavor. I also enjoy spicy heat, so I do like to add 1 to 2 teaspoons (2 to 4 g) of dried red pepper flakes,

although this is not necessary. Of course, fresh herbs such as basil or thyme leaves are a wonderful addition. Try adding ½ teaspoon of anise seed, which offers a slightly minty, sweet flavor that nicely balances the savory sauce. Be sure to season the sauce well with salt and pepper and give it a generous stir, making sure all the ingredients are well combined.

Partially cover with a lid and simmer for 1 hour, stirring from time to time, to allow all of the flavors to deepen and the sauce to thicken. Adjust the time depending on how thick you would like your sauce. The longer you simmer, the richer it will be. If you are in a hurry, you can remove it from the heat after simmering for 20 or 30 minutes, but I say the longer the better.

Remove the bay leaf and serve this with spaghetti with lots of Parmesan cheese for a traditional Sunday lunch.

Bolognese Sauce

Everyone loves a rich and tasty Bolognese sauce. It is a kind of ragu that originated in Bologna, Italy. The combination of ground beef, wine, garlic and herbs creates the foundation of a hearty sauce. Bolognese is perfect for those cold winter months, when you tuck in to a big bowl of pasta. I personally love to use thick tube-shaped pasta, such as rigatoni or penne, as the thick sauce gets caught in all the right spots, making each mouthful a delight!

I love to add some of Mum's Homemade Sugo di Pomodoro (page 14). It already has so much flavor, so when you combine the ingredients to make a Bolognese, it elevates the sauce to the next level. Starting with it as a base and then building it up to your taste is exactly what a true Italian does in their kitchen. I use this Bolognese recipe for lots of dishes, including lasagna, stuffed peppers and baked pasta. It is super versatile, not to mention delicious.

Traditional Bolognese has ground beef and pork, accompanied by red wine and beef stock, which is cooked down and simmered over low heat for 2 to 3 hours. In this recipe I use ground beef, but feel free to use a combination of beef and pork. I find beef and/or pork to be best for a ragu, although ground chicken or turkey would work if that's what you have on hand.

In this recipe I have added diced pancetta, as I love the saltiness it brings to the sauce. Depending on your taste preference, you can add 3.5 ounces (100 g) or more of pancetta, guanciale or bacon, although leaving this out would not be a deal breaker. Salted meat can really bring out the savoriness of the beef, creating a wonderful base and offering complementary flavors.

→ **Makes 67.6 oz (2 L)** ←

Ingredients

3.5 oz (100 g) pancetta, diced

¼ cup (60 ml) extra virgin olive oil

2 or 3 cloves garlic, roughly chopped

1 white onion, finely chopped

2 tbsp (30 g) butter

2 tbsp (30 g) tomato paste

2 carrots, peeled and diced small

2 ribs celery, finely chopped

1 lb (454 g) ground beef

½ cup (120 ml) red wine

2½ cups (600 ml) Mum's Homemade Sugo di Pomodoro (page 14)

½ cup (120 ml) beef stock

2 bay leaves

Salt and freshly ground black pepper

Method

In a large saucepan, add the pancetta and fry over low heat for 6 to 8 minutes, until golden and crispy. Pancetta offers a great amount of flavor, which is perfect in Bolognese. If you prefer, use another salted cured meat, such as guanciale or bacon.

Pour in the olive oil, then add the garlic and onion and cook for 2 to 3 minutes, until the onion is translucent. Add the butter and stir until melted. Stir in the tomato paste and cook for 1 to 2 minutes until it melts into the butter. Add in the carrots and celery. Cook for about 10 minutes until the vegetables start to soften, stirring occasionally.

Increase the heat to medium and add your choice of ground beef, pork, chicken or turkey. Adding ½ pound (226 g) each of two different types of meat, such as beef and pork, will work nicely too. Give it a good stir to prevent it from sticking to the bottom, and cook the meat for about 6 to 8 minutes, until it starts to brown. Pour in the red wine and allow a few minutes for the alcohol to cook off and for the liquid to reduce, about 2 to 3 minutes. Pour in Mum's Homemade Sugo di Pomodoro, the beef stock, bay leaves, salt and pepper, and stir gently to combine.

Since Bolognese gets so much flavor from the pancetta and meat, I like to keep it simple and season the sauce with just salt and pepper, but you could add your own touch of extra seasoning. Reduce the heat to low, cover and simmer for up to 2 to 3 hours, stirring occasionally, until the sauce thickens. Remove the bay leaves before serving.

Vegetarian Sauce

A traditional Bolognese is incredible, but if meat is not your thing, then you don't need to miss out on all the fun! Versatile with lots of fresh veggies, this twist on a classic makes a meat-free dinner and gives you the perfect opportunity to use up what you have in your kitchen or garden.

A great place to start is with vegetables such as carrots, onions and celery, like you would a traditional Bolognese. But don't stop there. I love to add in some zucchini and eggplant, which make the sauce rich and tasty. A 14-ounce (400-g) can of brown lentils, drained and rinsed, or 2 cups (140 g) of sliced white mushrooms are a lovely addition to the sauce, not to mention a hearty alternative to meat. A head of broccoli or cauliflower can also be substituted for the meat, just dice them into smaller pieces. When dicing the vegetables, make sure that they are all of equal size so they cook evenly.

Vegetables love seasoning, which is why I recommend you find a flavor combo you love with your choice of herbs and spices. Fresh or dried herbs such as thyme, oregano, basil, parsley and/or fennel seeds are tasty additions. Don't be afraid to experiment with the herbs and spices you have in your kitchen.

Ingredients

¼ cup (60 ml) extra virgin olive oil

1 white onion, finely chopped

2 or 3 cloves garlic, roughly chopped

1 carrot, finely diced

1 rib celery, finely diced

1 zucchini, diced into ½-inch (1.3-cm) cubes

1 eggplant, diced into ½-inch (1.3-cm) cubes

2 tbsp (30 g) butter

2 tbsp (30 g) tomato paste

2½ cups (600 ml) Mum's Homemade Sugo di Pomodoro (page 14)

1 (14-oz [400-g]) can brown lentils, drained and rinsed

1 or 2 bay leaves

1 tsp dried red pepper flakes (optional)

Salt and freshly ground black pepper

Method

Heat the olive oil in a large saucepan over low heat. Add the onion and garlic and cook for 2 to 3 minutes, until the onion is soft and translucent. Add the carrot and celery, stirring well, and fry the vegetables for 8 to 10 minutes until they become soft. Add any additional vegetables such as zucchini, eggplant, broccoli, cauliflower and potatoes, giving them a little time to soften.

Add the butter and tomato paste, allowing them to cook off for 1 to 2 minutes, until a little caramelized. Pour in Mum's Homemade Sugo di Pomodoro, then add the canned lentils, the bay leaves and your choice of herbs and spices, such as dried red pepper flakes, 1 teaspoon of oregano or thyme, or ½ teaspoon of fennel seeds.

Stir well to combine and season to taste with salt and pepper. As the vegetables don't require lots of time to cook like a traditional meat Bolognese, cover and simmer over low heat for 30 minutes, until the sauce thickens and the vegetables are soft. Remove the bay leaves before serving.

Hazelnut Pesto Sauce

The combination of fresh basil, Parmesan, garlic, nuts and olive oil creates the famous stunning green nutty sauce that originated in Liguria, Italy. With very few simple ingredients, pesto is one of those delicious sauces that not only can be changed to suit your taste buds but can also be used for multiple dishes, which makes it an absolute winner.

It is quite possibly one of the easiest midweek sauces that you can whip up. Pine nuts are traditional—they give off a wonderful mild buttery smell and when mixed with the other ingredients lend a sweet flavor. Of course you can use a different type of nut as an alternative, like I have in this recipe. Personally, I love the combination of the toasted hazelnuts crushed with the fresh basil and Parmesan cheese. Depending on the type of nut you add to your recipe, the taste of your pesto will change slightly. Almonds give a sweet and slightly bitter taste, whereas macadamia nuts provide a buttery richness. Unsalted pistachios have a sweet, earthy flavor that brings out the taste of the pesto even more. With any nut substitutions, I recommend sticking to the recipe amount of 1 cup (about 120 g) total as any more will cause the sauce to become rough in texture and unbalanced in flavor.

Instead of using just basil, you could add another leafy green vegetable such as baby spinach, Swiss chard or even kale to the mixture. Add 1 cup (30 g) of baby spinach to 1 cup (12 g) of basil leaves, to offer a balance of flavors.

I love to make this with freshly grated Parmesan, but other hard aged cheeses such as grana padano or pecorino Romano will work just as well. I personally love using pecorino Romano sometimes, which has a really bold taste.

Homemade pesto is one of the simplest sauces you can make in under 15 minutes. It can be added to pasta dishes, such as gnocchi, lasagna and penne, and can be served as a classic dip on its own or drizzled over roasted vegetables, pizza and grilled meats.

Ingredients

1 cup (120 g) raw hazelnuts

2 cups (24 g) fresh basil leaves, stems removed

⅓ cup (33 g) grated Parmesan cheese

2 cloves garlic, minced

½ cup (120 ml) extra virgin olive oil

1 tsp salt

Method

Preheat the oven to 350°F (175°C).

Pour the raw hazelnuts onto a large baking dish and put them into the oven to roast for 8 to 10 minutes, until they start to turn golden. Remove from the oven and set aside to cool slightly. Use a towel or your hands to gently remove the skins from the hazelnuts. It doesn't need to be perfect—just try to get most of the skin off.

Once the skins have been removed, add the toasted hazelnuts to a food processor. If you are using another alternative such as almonds, walnuts, pistachios, macadamias or traditional pine nuts, you can add them directly into the food processor, as they will not need to be roasted.

Add the basil leaves, Parmesan cheese and garlic to the food processor with the nuts, and pulse a few times until all the ingredients are chopped small. Scrape down the sides of the food processor, if needed.

While the food processor is running, slowly add the olive oil in a thin stream. As you pour in the oil, the pesto will come together to form a smooth sauce, which is exactly what you are looking for. If the pesto seems too thick, you can add a little bit more oil until you get the consistency you like. Add the salt—feel free to adjust the amount according to your taste.

Use the pesto sauce on some freshly cooked homemade pasta (page 24) or drizzle over the base of a homemade focaccia (page 122).

Pepe Arrostiti

Making *pepe arrostiti* (roasted peppers) is my absolute favorite thing to do. The traditional way of roasting peppers is over an open burner on top of a gas stove. The smoky smell and peppery taste are exceptional, and these roasted peppers can be added to many dishes, but I think they taste the best when spread over fresh ciabatta.

I prefer roasting bell peppers over an open stovetop burner, as it adds so much flavor. If you have an electric stovetop, you can roast them in the oven. You could even try placing the peppers on a sheet pan under the broiler. Keep an eye on them, as they can go from nicely charred to scorched quite quickly; turn occasionally so the whole pepper is charred. In this recipe, I've given advice for both cooking methods: the traditional way of roasting peppers and the more modern oven-roasting method. If you've never roasted peppers the traditional Italian way, I urge you to give it a red-hot go, and I predict it will be the method you follow going forward.

I use a mix of different peppers, as I love the bright gorgeous colors, but choose what you like. Red, yellow and orange peppers are quite sweet, so I like to use a variety of these types. Using pimento peppers is a great way to add a little sweetness. There are also many different varieties of peppers that you can char on an open flame. Pepperoncini and jalapeño have a noticeable kick, so be mindful of this when adding the herbs and spices.

Because the peppers are roasted on an open flame, they have lots of flavor already, so I add very little seasoning, as I don't want to lose any of that charred taste. I stick to traditional ingredients such as thinly sliced garlic, fresh parsley and extra virgin olive oil. Of course, adding fresh basil or oregano or a fresh chile is fine.

Keep the Pepe Arrostiti refrigerated in an airtight container for up to 3 months. The oil helps to preserve them, and they can be added to my Fresh & Simple Bruschetta (page 116), Grilled Vegetable Pizza (page 80) or Panzanella (page 132).

Ingredients

8 bell peppers (mix of red, orange and yellow)

½ cup (120 ml) extra virgin olive oil

2 cloves garlic, finely sliced

A handful of fresh parsley, roughly chopped

Salt

Method

Rinse the bell peppers in water and dry them well prior to roasting or grilling. Heat the largest burner on your stovetop. If you have an electric stovetop, follow the oven method below.

Depending on the size of your burner, put 1 or 2 peppers directly over the flame. A warning: This method can get a little messy, as the peppers may leak onto your burner, so please watch them very carefully. Once they're charred and blistered, turn them over to char the other side. Repeat this process for the remaining peppers.

To roast them in the oven, preheat the oven to 425°F (220°C). Place the peppers 1 inch (2.5 cm) apart on a nonstick baking sheet, and put the baking sheet in the oven. Use tongs to rotate them when one side has blistered and charred, making sure it has completely charred all over, roughly 25 minutes.

For either method, once the peppers are completely charred, put them into a large bowl and cover with plastic wrap. The residual heat will help remove the skin from the flesh of the peppers, making it so much easier to peel. Keep it covered for 15 to 20 minutes, until the peppers are cool enough to touch.

Once cool enough to handle, remove the seeds, membranes and outer skin. They should peel easily, but don't fret if all of the skin doesn't come off. Put the peppers onto a cutting board and slice them into thin strips, then transfer them to a clean bowl. Pour in the olive oil and sliced garlic and season with your choice of herbs and the salt. I've kept it simple with freshly chopped parsley, but you could add fresh basil leaves, oregano or dried red pepper flakes.

Serve the Pepe Arrostiti on a large platter with serving forks and plenty of fresh ciabatta.

Homemade Pasta

Making excessively large amounts of pasta is what Italians do very well, and my family is definitely no different. Growing up making fresh pasta was a tradition in which the whole family would lend a hand to help make lunch for that day.

My recipes in this cookbook use a mixture of homemade and store-bought pasta, although you can make any one of these pastas with a sauce from any one of the recipes listed. Italian cooking is all about being creative with what you have on hand.

Semolina is the traditional flour for a sturdy pasta dough, perfect for handmade shapes such as orecchiette (page 28) and cavatelli (page 30). Keeping the pasta light is key, which is why I love using a finer semolina flour as it helps the pasta to retain its shape. You can most definitely replace the semolina with Tipo 00 plain flour or all-purpose flour if needed. Tipo 00 plain flour is a type of flour that is milled in Italy. It is a fine-grade flour typically used in pasta making. In most of these recipes, I have used a combination of 3 cups (500 g) of semolina and 1 cup (125 g) of Tipo 00 plain flour, as the combination helps to craft sturdy pasta shapes. In some dishes polenta can be substituted for semolina, but in pasta, I would not recommend it. Polenta is a type of corn flour that has a completely different texture, and when it's boiled in water it disintegrates, creating a gooey mess.

Traditional egg pasta is well-known in the northern regions of Italy such as Emilia-Romagna and Tuscany. Incorporating eggs into the flour enriches the dough, which creates a deliciously silky texture and a rich flavor. Fettuccine (page 35), ravioli and pappardelle (page 36) all include eggs. If you're serious about pasta making and want to make it a regular thing, I recommend investing in a good-quality pasta-making machine. There are many great ones available that are perfect for the beginner or expert. Of course, you can make the pasta by hand, but if you lack time and want instant results, a pasta machine is definitely the way to go.

In terms of substitutions, the same notes for the semolina dough applies to making egg pasta. Keep it fairly straightforward with 4 cups (500 g) of Tipo 00 plain flour or all-purpose flour. The key to getting a really golden rich color in the pasta is all the egg yolks, so by adding more egg yolks than whole, you create moisture for the gluten to work its magic, which enriches the dough.

I have seen many homemade pasta recipes with added flavors that create a fun approach to pasta. Ingredients such as black squid ink, basil, beetroot, carrot and spinach all have incredible tastes and look beautiful when rolled out into shapes. Some of these ingredients are cooked first, if needed (such as beetroot, carrot or spinach), then pureed in a food processor and added to the remaining pasta ingredients. Experiment with a pasta machine by using the different settings to make fresh pasta dough for lasagna or fettuccine. There is so much joy in making pasta.

Semolina Pasta Dough

⇒ **Makes 2 lb (1 kg)** ⇐

Ingredients

3 cups (500 g) semolina flour

1 cup (125 g) Tipo 00 plain flour or all-purpose flour

1 tsp salt

1½ cups (360 ml) water

Method

Working on a clean surface, pour out the semolina flour, Tipo 00 plain flour and salt, and use your hands to make a little well in the center of the flour. Slowly pour the water into the center and use a fork to slowly combine the wet and dry ingredients, until they start to form a dough. Personally, I love working with my hands, but if you're short on time, you can use a stand mixer as well.

Keep an eye on the consistency of the dough, and add either a little more flour or water if it's too wet or too dry. A rough, coarse texture where the dough is not sticking together would require a little more water to help bind the dough. If your dough is extremely wet and sticking to the surface you're working on, then adding flour a little at a time as you're kneading will help it come together.

Once the dough has come together, begin to knead it on a lightly floured surface for about 10 minutes. While kneading, you'll begin to notice that the dough will start to feel smooth between your hands, which is the exact consistency you're looking for.

Once kneaded, shape the dough into a ball, wrap tightly in plastic wrap, cover with a tea towel and allow to rest for 30 minutes. Some people skip this step, but it's important that you allow the dough to rest in order for the gluten in the flour to relax. Relaxing the dough will help you easily shape the pasta. Once the dough has rested, proceed to create your choice of pasta shapes. Recipes for orecchiette (page 28) and cavatelli (page 30), two of my favorites and some of the easiest handmade pasta shapes, follow.

*See step-by-step images over the following pages, where my mother is using the traditional method of making homemade pasta from scratch.

Semolina Pasta Dough (Continued)

1. Pour both flours and the salt onto a clean work surface.

2. Use your hands to make a well in the center of the flour.

3. Pour the water in and use a fork to slowly start to combine the ingredients together.

4. Work the dough with your hands to combine.

5. Use your hands to strongly knead your dough as this step is important. Or alternatively you can use a stand mixer to combine and knead.

6. Continue kneading and make sure your dough is combined well in order for the dough to be a smooth consistency; this will allow you to create your desired shapes. Once it is smooth, wrap and allow to rest for 30 minutes.

Orecchiette

Orecchiette originated in Puglia, in the southern region of Italy. *Orecchiette*, which means "little ears" in Italian, can be a little tricky to get the hang of it at first, but with some practice, you'll be making gorgeous homemade orecchiette in no time.

Ingredients
Semolina Pasta Dough (page 25)

Method

Lightly flour a clean surface with a little semolina, and divide the rested dough into four equal pieces. Put one piece of dough in the middle of your work surface, and cover the remaining pieces with a damp tea towel or plastic wrap. Using your hands, roll out the piece of dough into a 12-inch (30-cm) log shape.

Cut the log into smaller pieces, about ½ inch (1.3 cm) or roughly the same size. Taking one small piece at a time, and with a blunt knife, gently press down and in one motion drag the knife toward you. The dough will wrap and curl under the knife. Use your thumb to gently turn the dough in the opposite direction to form a concave shape, exposing the rough side. Put the orecchiette on a large cutting board or tea towel with a light sprinkle of semolina and repeat with the remaining dough until it's all been used. Cover the orecchiette with a damp towel to prevent it from drying out.

To cook the orecchiette, put them in a large pot of salted boiling water. Gently stir to prevent them from sticking to the bottom. They will rise to the surface almost immediately. Allow them to boil for 2 to 3 minutes before draining and adding to the sauce of your choice.

1. Roll a piece of dough into a log shape and cut it into roughly ½-inch (1.3-cm) pieces in preparation to create your orecchiette.

2. Working with one piece at a time, use a blunt knife to gently press down on a piece of dough.

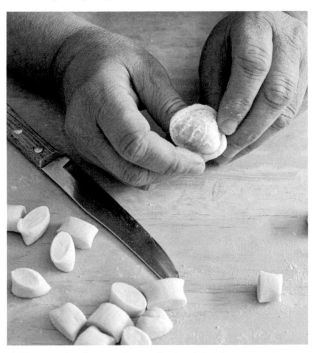

3. In one motion, gently drag the knife towards you. The dough will gather and curl underneath the knife.

4. Use your thumb to gently turn the dough inside out, creating a concave shape and exposing the rough side.

Cavatelli

Cavatelli, or "little hollows," come from the southern region of Italy—Puglia, Basilicata and Calabria—and there are several ways to make them. My family is from the town of Paterno in Basilicata, and our more rustic version has a similar method to creating the popular cavatelli shape, just with the technique being slightly different. It involves taking a larger piece of dough and using your index, middle and ring fingers to drag the dough toward you, creating a larger, rustic ear shape with a thicker edge. This type of cavatelli is quite common from my hometown in Italy, but the more popular way of making cavatelli is in the recipe which follows. When making your own cavatelli, you may try either method.

Another method is to use a smaller piece of dough placed on the base of a gnocchi board and then use your thumb to drag the dough away from your body. These resemble the shape of gnocchi but with a concave center that soaks up all the sauce.

Ingredients
Semolina Pasta Dough (page 25)

Method

As with the orecchiette, lightly flour a clean surface with semolina and divide the rested dough into four equal pieces. Put one piece of dough in the middle of your work surface, and cover the remaining pieces with a damp tea towel or plastic wrap. With your hands, roll out the piece of dough into a 12-inch (30-cm) log shape.

Cut off 1- to 1½-inch (2.5- to 4-cm) pieces and, one piece at a time, press down on the dough using your index and middle fingers (or also use your ring finger as my family does), and then slowly drag the dough toward you, creating an indent or concave shape.

Another way of creating a similar shape would be to use a gnocchi board, as mentioned above. As you're dragging the dough, it will create indented lines on the opposite side, which allows the sauce to attach to it. Please note: You do not necessarily need a gnocchi board for this method, but it's a great way to get creative in making your own interesting shapes and styles.

Put the cavatelli on a large cutting board or tea towel with a light sprinkle of semolina and repeat with the remaining dough until it's all been used. Cover with a damp towel to prevent from drying out.

To cook the cavatelli, carefully add them to a large pot of salted boiling water. Gently stir to prevent them from sticking to the bottom. They will rise to the surface almost immediately. Allow them to boil for 2 to 3 minutes before draining and adding to the sauce of your choice.

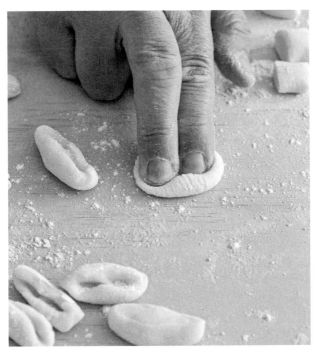

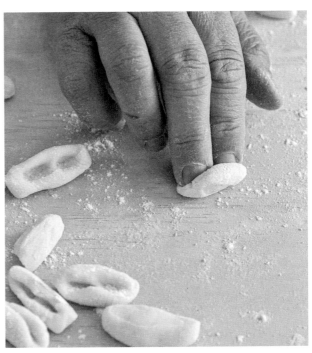

1. Gently press your index and middle finger into each piece of dough.

2. In a similar motion to using a knife, drag the dough toward you, creating a concave shape.

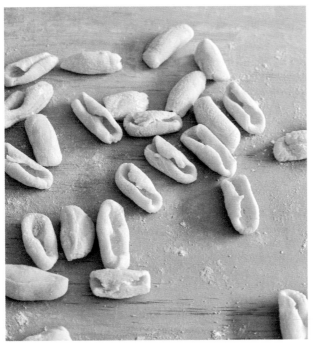

3. Repeat the process with all the remaining pieces of dough until all have been used.

4. Try this method using a gnocchi board by following the same steps, starting from the base and dragging the dough toward you.

Egg Pasta Dough

→ **Makes 2 lb (1 kg)** ←

Ingredients

4 cups (500 g) Tipo 00 plain flour or all-purpose flour

1 tsp salt

5 whole eggs

2 egg yolks

1 tbsp (15 ml) extra virgin olive oil

Method

Put the flour and salt onto a clean surface and make a well in the center.

Crack your eggs one at a time into a bowl and add them to the center of the well. My nonna does it this way to reduce the risk of adding a bad egg to the mixture. Add the olive oil to the well and use a fork to beat the eggs, then slowly incorporate the eggs and oil with the flour.

Once the dough has come together, knead the dough for 10 minutes. Like the semolina pasta dough, it should be soft and smooth between your hands. Wrap in plastic and refrigerate for 30 minutes.

1. On a clean work surface, pour your flour and salt. Use your hand to make a well in the center of the flour.

2. Pour in your eggs and oil and use a fork to gently start to combine them with the flour.

3. Once the eggs and flour have started to incorporate together, take over the process using your hands.

4. Knead the dough with your hands to achieve a smooth and soft consistency. Wrap and allow the dough to rest for 30 minutes.

The Complete Italian Essentials ➔ **33**

5. Once the dough has rested, divide it into four pieces. Use a rolling pin to prepare the dough for the pasta machine.

6. Feed the pieces of dough through your pasta machine, starting at the widest setting.

7. Work the dough through each of the settings, starting with the widest and ending with the thinnest setting.

8. Feed the thin sheet of dough through the pasta machine one last time, using the cutting attachment of your choice.

Fettuccine

Fettuccine ("little ribbons") are flat ribbon-shaped pasta, used in recipes such as carbonara and alfredo. The beautiful silky strands are bright in color and taste delicious with my puttanesca sauce (page 60).

Ingredients

Egg Pasta Dough (page 32)

Method

Divide the dough into four equal pieces, and, working with one piece at a time, dust a little flour over the dough and use a rolling pin to slightly flatten it. This will help when feeding it through the pasta machine. Set up your pasta machine, and, starting with the widest setting, roll the dough through and lay it flat on a lightly floured surface. Fold the dough by bringing in each of the sides to the center, then fold it again to form the shape of a rectangle. This will help keep a consistent shape when feeding it through the machine.

Repeat this method about three times on the widest setting and then work your way down to the thinnest setting, feeding the pasta sheet through. If you're making lasagna, roll it out on the third-to-last setting, as this creates the perfect thickness. You should end up with a relatively long sheet of dough that is thin enough to be worked with but delicate enough that it can break, so please be gentle. Put the pasta on tea towels with a little flour to prevent it from drying out.

If the sheets of pasta have become too long to work with, it's perfectly fine to cut them in half. Using the fettuccine cutter attachment on your pasta machine, feed the sheet in, catching it as you move the pasta through. After the pasta has come through the machine, shape them into little bundles and lay them on a lightly floured surface. Sprinkle them with a little semolina flour to prevent them from sticking. Repeat with the remaining dough until all of it has been used.

To cook your homemade fettuccine, carefully add them to a large pot of salted boiling water. Gently stir to prevent them from sticking to the bottom. They will rise to the surface almost immediately. Allow them to boil for 2 to 3 minutes before draining and adding to the sauce of your choice.

Pappardelle

Pappardelle are thick-cut ribbons that are sensational with rich, deep sauces. The name *pappardelle* comes from the word *pappare*, which means "to gobble up"—which is exactly what happens when you have a large plate in front of you. These lovely egg ribbons are fabulous with a hearty ragu or a creamy mushroom sauce.

Ingredients

Egg Pasta Dough (page 32)

Method

Divide the dough into four equal pieces. Dust a little semolina on the dough you are working with, then use a rolling pin to flatten it slightly. Feed the dough through the highest setting on the pasta machine and fold the sheet into the center and then into a rectangle. Repeat this method about three times on the widest setting and then work your way down to the thinnest setting.

Depending on the length of your dough, cut into 10- to 12-inch (25- to 30-cm) sheets and roll each piece loosely. Slice into 1-inch (2.5-cm) pappardelle strips. Dust a little semolina flour and leave them to dry on tea towels. Repeat with the remaining dough until it all has been used.

To cook the pappardelle, carefully add them into a large pot of salted boiling water. Gently stir to prevent them from sticking to the bottom. They will rise to the surface almost immediately. Allow them to boil for 2 to 3 minutes before draining and adding to the sauce of your choice.

1. Gently fold your rolled out pieces of dough in preparation to cut into pappardelle strands.

2. Using your knife, slice the dough into 1-inch (2.5-cm) pieces, making sure they are relatively the same in size.

3. Lightly coat your pappardelle with a little flour to prevent them from sticking together.

4. Place the pappardelle on a lightly floured surface, giving them enough space to slightly dry.

Homemade Pizza Dough

Eating Nonna's famous Margherita pizza on the weekends is one of my favorite childhood memories. It would amaze me how she would get it exactly the same each time she made it. When it came out of the oven, the house would be completely filled with the incredible smell of pizza. It's still one of my favorite things to this day.

Now that Nonna is in her eighties, her delicious pizzas are becoming less frequent, but I had the opportunity to sit with her so she could pass on her recipe. Not the typical thin-crust pizza you see in restaurants today, our family's recipe has a slightly thicker base. This dough is used for making pizza and calzones. It is a method she has used since she was very young. I feel that rolling out the dough with a rolling pin flattens it substantially, which is why I like to keep it relatively thick. Feel free to experiment with different techniques to find one that suits your preference.

Using fresh yeast in the recipe is what makes this dough shine. It is considered richer and has a better rising quality than dried yeast. Of course, if you're unable to find fresh yeast, dried yeast will work just as well. Please be mindful that using too much yeast can cause the dough to rise quickly only to become flat.

Judge whether the last ¼ cup (60 ml) of warm water is necessary, based on the texture of your dough. Overworking or underworking the dough is another important factor, as you want to get the right consistency. If you press down on your dough and it springs back, your dough is ready. Give the dough enough time to rest in a warm, dark place. A maximum of 2 hours should be enough for the dough to rise completely.

Bake your pizzas in the oven at 400°F (200°C) for 30 to 35 minutes, depending on your oven. If you have a pizza oven, pop these in for half the amount of cooking time, as they will cook quicker. This recipe makes one large pizza base, or you can divide it in half to make two smaller bases. If you are making multiple pizzas, this recipe can be doubled. Making pizza together is a fun (and delicious) way to have family time.

→ **Makes 1 large pizza base or 2 smaller bases** ←

Ingredients

½ oz (14 g) fresh yeast or 1¾ tsp (7 g) dried yeast

1¼ cups (300 ml) warm water, divided

1 lb (454 g) all-purpose flour or strong bread flour, plus 3½ tbsp (45 g) for dusting

½ tsp salt

3–4 tbsp (45–60 ml) extra virgin olive oil, divided

Method

Add the fresh yeast to about 1 cup (240 ml) of warm water and, using a fork, whisk until it has completely dissolved. Repeat the same process if using dried yeast. Let the mixture sit for 5 to 10 minutes or until small bubbles appear on the surface. Pour the flour and salt onto a clean surface and make a well in the center. Pour the water and yeast into the center of the well, and use your hands to mix the ingredients together.

Adjust the consistency of the dough by using the remaining ¼ cup (60 ml) of warm water. This is where you will have to use your instincts and senses to achieve the right consistency. If the dough is a little dry, add a little water. If the mixture becomes too wet, use a little flour to lightly coat your hands. You will need to rely on your sense of touch and adjust accordingly. The dough should feel easy for you to work with. Knead the dough for 10 minutes. When ready, it will feel soft and elastic and will spring back when pressed down.

Transfer the dough to a large bowl that will allow enough room for it to rise. Cover the bowl with plastic wrap and two tea towels. The towels create a little heat bubble, which helps the dough to expand. Place the dough in a dark place at room temperature to rest. About 30 minutes into resting, remove the towels and plastic wrap and use your hands to gently knock the air out of the dough. Cover it back up with plastic wrap and towels, and pop it back in the dark spot and allow to rise for 1½ to 2 hours, until it has doubled in size.

Once the dough has doubled in size, remove it from the bowl and put it on a clean, lightly floured surface. With this amount of dough, you can easily make one large pizza or two smaller pizza bases.

To prepare your pizza for the oven, lightly coat a 12 x 18–inch (30 x 45–cm) baking sheet with a good amount of olive oil. My family has only ever used standard baking pans when making pizzas, but today there is a great selection to choose from. Cast-iron pizza pans are extremely versatile and can be used in the oven, under the broiler or on the stove top. Pizza stones are also very popular. The stone helps make the crust extra crispy while it bakes. You can also try different shapes of trays, including rectangular, round or square.

Lightly cover your hands with a little extra virgin olive oil and gently stretch out the dough. Slowly pull out the dough using your fingertips to cover the base of the tray. I prefer the rustic look when it comes to making pizza, and pulling the dough with your hands achieves this result. Alternatively, you can use a rolling pin to achieve a flat round surface if you prefer, but you will not achieve the same level of thickness as you would when stretching the dough with your hands.

Use your fingertips to gently make little dimples on the surface of the dough, being careful not to dig through the bottom of the dough. Drizzle a little olive oil over the top, and spread it evenly with your hands. There is no need to be perfect with this—the more rustic the better, I say!

Now comes the best part, adding the toppings! The key is to be creative and intuitive, focusing on which flavors work really well together. The recipes in chapter three (pages 71 to 85) showcase a few of my favorites, but feel free to create your own.

*See step-by-step images on the following pages.

Homemade Pizza Dough (Continued)

1. *Prepare the flour, yeast, salt and water on a large clean surface.*

2. *Pour the flour and salt into a large bowl and make a well in the center with your hand.*

3. *Pour the yeast mixed with the warm water into the center of the well.*

4. *Use your hands to mix all the ingredients together, making sure they are well combined.*

5. Transfer the dough to a clean work surface and use your hands to start to knead the dough.

6. Continue kneading until you have a smooth consistency, then place the dough into a bowl to rise until it has doubled in size.

7. Remove the risen dough from the bowl and lightly coat with a little flour just before transferring it to a lightly oiled baking sheet.

8. Use your fingertips to stretch out the dough over the oiled baking sheet.

Rustic Italian Bread

I really don't think there is anything better than the intoxicating smell of fresh-baked bread. Eating a slice of rustic bread smothered in butter is my idea of heaven. Bread is a consistent staple found on all Italian tables at meal times. Don't listen to anyone who tells you not to fill up on bread before a meal. You don't need that kind of negativity in your life!

With a similar preparation process to making a pizza, bread actually requires even less effort on your part. No kneading! The key to successful bread depends on how you activate the yeast. You want to make sure that the water is neither too hot nor cold. I don't really use any type of particular method when doing this, but if you're not too sure, use a thermometer to get the right temperature before adding it into the mix. You're looking for 110°F (45°C) to get the right texture and consistency. (A higher temperature will kill the yeast.)

You can add whatever flavors you prefer to the dough. If you like garlic, mince 2 or 3 cloves and add them at the beginning. If using herbs, such as rosemary, thyme or basil, add roughly 1 to 2 tablespoons (about 2 g) into the bowl before combining all the ingredients together.

I love grated Parmesan cheese in anything, so why not add it to your dough? Grate ½ cup (50 g) of Parmesan, and add it to the mixture. I suggest sticking to fairly hard cheeses such as pecorino or Parmesan, as they will work better with the dough than a softer cheese such as mozzarella or ricotta, which will add too much moisture.

Bread flour is best suited for this recipe, as it contains a higher protein content than other types and will give you great results. It creates a soft and fluffy inside with a crunchy outer edge. Of course, bread flour is not a necessity, so all-purpose flour can be used. You can eat this bread on its own or use it in a variety of different recipes, such the a base for my Fresh & Simple Bruschetta (page 116). If there is any bread left, and I'm sure there won't be, you can also tear up a few slices and turn them into croutons for my Panzanella (page 132) or use it for the filling in my Italian Meatballs Three Ways (page 93).

→ **Makes 1 loaf** ←

Ingredients

3¼ cups (445 g) bread flour or all-purpose flour, plus more for shaping

2 tsp (11 g) salt

1 tsp granulated sugar

1¾ tsp (7 g) dried yeast

1½ cups (360 ml) lukewarm water

1 tsp extra virgin olive oil

Method

In a large bowl, add the flour, salt, sugar and yeast, and whisk the ingredients until they are well mixed. At this point, mix in any alternative ingredients if you are using them—minced garlic, rosemary, basil, thyme or cheese. Pour in the lukewarm water and olive oil and use a wooden spoon to stir until the dough looks shaggy but mixed together, for roughly 1 or 2 minutes. The dough will be quite sticky and wet, which is exactly the consistency you want.

Cover the dough with plastic wrap and a tea towel and set aside in a dark place to rest at room temperature for 12 hours or overnight. The dough will rise and form little bubbles on the top. As the dough has a long rise, it will not need to rise again and can be put right into the oven.

Preheat the oven to 450°F (230°C) and heat a cast-iron pot or Dutch oven inside for 20 to 25 minutes. While the oven and pot are heating, dust a sheet of parchment paper generously with flour. With well-floured hands, remove the dough from the bowl, put it onto the parchment paper, and shape the dough into a ball. Dust a little more flour over the top and allow it to sit while the pot heats in the oven.

Carefully remove the pot from the oven and remove the lid. With extreme care, transfer the parchment paper with the dough into the pot. Put the lid back on and put the pot back into the oven. Bake for 30 to 35 minutes. Remove the lid and bake uncovered for another 10 to 15 minutes, until the dough is baked through and the top of the loaf is golden brown.

Once cooked, remove the pot from the oven, and allow the bread to rest in the pot for about 15 minutes. Turn the loaf out onto a wire rack to cool. Cut the bread into thick slices and serve with a generous amount of butter or any toppings you'd like.

Chapter Two

Pasta Perfetto

When I think about pasta, it really does make me smile. When I traveled to my hometown of Paterno in Basilicata, I was mesmerized by the way my family would create a homemade pasta dish in a matter of minutes. It was made so effortlessly and authentically that it made me fall in love with the process even more. It inspired me to replicate these dishes at home, creating my own unique versions and experimenting with flavors.

Whether the pasta is dried or freshly made, it is the simplicity of this readily available ingredient that makes it versatile. It is without a doubt one of my most favorite things to use in the kitchen. The recipes in this chapter use dried pasta, but if you want to experiment and master your pasta-making skills, see my recipes for homemade pasta beginning on page 24. Please feel free to use those with any one of these dishes. Nothing is off-limits when it comes to eating pasta.

In this chapter, I explore traditional recipes and some exciting new ones with amazing, bold flavors to tantalize your taste buds and inspire you to create your own twists. These pasta recipes are not only adaptable but can also be used with other dishes in this book. Orecchiette with Broccoli & Sausages (page 58) can be adapted to a vegetarian delight using chickpeas, or you could try adding some fresh fennel in my Spaghetti alle Vongole (page 46). I share a traditional Rotolo di Spinaci (page 48) filled with ricotta and spinach, to which you can add cooked sweet potato or butternut squash with fresh mozzarella for a hearty, extra-cheesy version.

For me, pasta is something that really does bring a family together. It creates a familiar environment that provides comfort and love. As I always say, there is nothing that a large bowl of pasta can't fix!

Spaghetti alle Vongole

There are so many different takes on this fresh *vongole* ("clam") dish from southern Italy, but I absolutely love this one with very few ingredients. It packs a big flavor punch. It originated in the southern seaside region of Naples, but it is widely found throughout the country. Italians have two different versions of this dish—with tomatoes and without. I've tried both and can agree that they are both equally delicious. My recipe is a take on the *in bianco* (white sauce) variation, adding some brightness that comes from the juice and zest of a lemon and some heat from dried red pepper flakes.

I add fresh chile or dried red pepper flakes to many of my dishes, as I love the extra heat. However, if you want just a little heat in the dish, I suggest adding ½ teaspoon or perhaps a whole fresh mild chile, seeded and finely chopped, instead of the dried red pepper flakes. Adding lemon zest while the vongole are simmering adds a tartness that complements them nicely. A dry white wine, such as pinot grigio, adds a crisp, clean taste and works well with seafood.

I am a big fan of using fresh herbs in this dish, as they really bring the seafood to life. Of course, you can use dried parsley or basil, but it won't have the same taste fresh herbs provide. Try to use fresh herbs whenever possible. For an extra boost of flavor, try adding some thinly sliced fennel when you fry the garlic. Italians are renowned for using up every part of the vegetable, so even the fennel fronds can be included. Give the fronds a rough chop and toss them in with the parsley at the very end. If you want to use fresh tomatoes, roughly chop a few ripe ones and add them during the last 5 to 10 minutes of cooking.

Traditional alle vongole is used with long thin types of pasta, so instead of spaghetti some fantastic alternatives can include linguine, pici or fettucine pasta which would be lovely. These types of pastas soak up all the gorgeous flavors which have been created by the simmering sauce.

Ingredients

2 lb (1 kg) clams

½ cup (120 ml) extra virgin olive oil, plus more for serving

4 cloves garlic, finely diced

1 tsp dried red pepper flakes or ½ to 1 fresh mild chile, seeded and finely chopped (optional)

½ cup (120 ml) dry white wine

Zest and juice of 1 lemon, divided

1 lb (454 g) dried spaghetti or 1 batch Egg Pasta Dough (page 32), rolled and cut into spaghetti

Salt

½ cup (30 g) fresh flat-leaf parsley, finely chopped, plus more for serving

Method

Prepare the clams by submerging them in water for 20 minutes. Drain and repeat two to three times to remove any excess sand, discarding any that have been crushed or damaged. Set the cleaned clams aside in a colander while you prepare the remaining ingredients.

In a large saucepan, heat the olive oil over low heat and cook the garlic for 1 to 2 minutes, until fragrant. Stir in the red pepper flakes, if using, and increase the heat slightly. Add the clams to the saucepan, and give the pan a little shake to help cover the clams with the oil.

Pour in the white wine and allow it to simmer for a few minutes so the alcohol cooks off. Add the lemon zest, then squeeze the juice from one half of the lemon over the pan and give the clams another gentle toss. Reduce the heat and simmer for 8 to 10 minutes to allow the clams to open, stirring every few minutes. Discard any that haven't opened.

While the clams are simmering, bring a large pot of salted water to boil. Add the spaghetti and cook it to just al dente, about 2 to 3 minutes if using homemade. Fresh pasta cooks faster than dried pasta. When ready, drain and add the pasta to the clams.

Season with salt and add the fresh parsley or any other herbs or spices, such as fennel fronds. Squeeze the juice from the remaining lemon half and give the pasta a good toss, making sure it is coated completely in sauce. If you would like to add some fresh tomatoes, do so during the last 5 to 10 minutes of cooking, so they retain their shape and fresh taste.

Serve on a large platter sprinkled with finely chopped parsley, if desired, and a generous drizzle of extra virgin olive oil.

Rotolo di Spinaci

Popular in the Emilia-Romagna region, rotolo di spinaci is made from thinly rolled egg pasta that's filled with creamy ricotta, spinach and lemon. It is then wrapped tightly in a clean tea towel and boiled in a water bath. The roll is then sliced, placed into a baking dish and baked with grated cheese until golden.

It is an impressive dish, to say the least. Rolling the pasta with the tea towel may require a little practice, but it will be a showstopper. Make my Egg Pasta Dough (page 32) for a quick and easy pasta dough or, if you're strapped for time, fresh lasagna sheets will work just as well. Ten to twelve sheets will be enough for this dish, or depending on their size, you may need more. You will need to overlap these to create one large sheet.

The filling of a rotolo di spinaci is subjective, and you can create your own flavor combinations. I have used frozen spinach, but using fresh spinach or another leafy green such as Swiss chard or kale can be a wonderful alternative. Cut the greens into ½-inch (1.3-cm) pieces, add to a saucepan with a little extra virgin olive oil and salt and pepper, and cook them until wilted, about 2 to 3 minutes. When completely cool, add them to the ricotta filling. Adding about ½ cup (27 g) of sun-dried tomatoes, roughly chopped, would give the filling an extra level of tartness.

You can also dice ½ pumpkin, 1 sweet potato or 1 butternut squash and roast it in the oven for 25 to 30 minutes until soft. Gently mash, and once cooled, add it to the cheesy mixture. I love to sprinkle grated mozzarella and Parmesan over the top of the dish before popping it into the oven.

Ingredients

1 batch Egg Pasta Dough (page 32) or 10–12 fresh or dried lasagna sheets

1 lb (454 g) frozen spinach, thawed and excess water squeezed out

1 lb (454 g) fresh ricotta cheese

1½ cups (168 g) shredded mozzarella cheese, divided

2 eggs

Salt and freshly ground black pepper

3 cups (720 ml) Mum's Homemade Sugo di Pomodoro (page 14), plus more if required

¾ cup (75 g) grated Parmesan cheese

Fresh basil leaves, for garnish

Method

Preheat the oven to 350°F (175°C).

While the pasta dough is resting, make the filling. In a large bowl, add the spinach, ricotta, 1 cup (112 g) of shredded mozzarella and the eggs. Add the salt and pepper and mix until all the ingredients are combined. If you'd like to use roasted pumpkin or sweet potato, season with a little salt and pepper and roast in the oven for 25 to 30 minutes until soft. Allow it to cool completely before mashing and adding to the ricotta mixture. Alternatively, if using different leafy greens, sauté in a saucepan with a little olive oil until wilted; once cooled, add them to the cheese mixture.

If you are using fresh pasta, roll it out to a thickness of ¹⁄₁₀ inch (2.5 mm). Cut the sheets to the length of your clean tea towel—you will probably fit two sheets on a standard-sized tea towel. Overlap the edges slightly and use a little water to help the edges stick together. If you are using store-bought fresh lasagna sheets, use as many sheets as needed to cover your tea towel, remembering to slightly overlap the edges and use a little water to secure them. If you cannot find fresh lasagna sheets, dried sheets will work just as well. Boil them in salted water, cooking them just under the recommended time, drain and lay them flat on a moist tea towel to prevent them from drying out.

Spread the filling all over the pasta sheets, leaving an inch (2.5 cm) at the end that is farthest away from you. This is to help fold over the roll so it can be secured into place. Brush this end with a little water. You may need a helping hand to roll up the dough. Starting at the edge closest to you, roll the pasta carefully, using your tea towel to roll away from you.

(continued)

Rotolo di Spinaci (Continued)

Once you reach the end, roll the tea towel right around the pasta, tying up each end firmly with a cooking string. This secures the sausage shape and ensures that the filling will not spill out. To secure even further, tie another piece of cooking string around the center. Bring a large pot of salted water to a boil. Gently submerge the rotolo into the water. You are poaching this, so you want to make sure it is kept completely covered by the water. Weighing it down with a plate on top of the parcel will help it stay completely submerged. Simmer for about 25 minutes. Carefully remove the rotolo from the water, and place it onto a large baking sheet. This is to allow the excess water from the tea towel to fall onto the tray. Let the rotolo cool just enough to handle in the tea towel prior to slicing.

Pour a layer of Mum's Homemade Sugo di Pomodoro all over the base of a 13 x 9–inch (33 x 23–cm) baking dish, reserving some to pour over the top. Once the rotolo has cooled enough to comfortably handle, cut it into ½-inch (1.3-cm) slices and put them into a single layer in the baking dish. Spoon the remaining sauce over the pasta and sprinkle the remaining mozzarella and all the grated Parmesan cheese all over the top. Bake for 20 to 25 minutes, until the cheese has melted and turns golden brown. Once cooked, allow to stand for 10 minutes prior to serving.

Garnish with fresh basil leaves and serve with a leafy green salad.

Hearty Minestrone

Have you ever had a wonderfully full-flavored soup that hits the spot each and every time you make it? Minestrone is a versatile vegetable soup that you can make with whatever ingredients you have on hand. It's a great way to use up all those sad-looking leftover veggies in your fridge. The soup takes a little time to prepare, but it's worth it.

You can tailor minestrone to your own personal taste. My nonna would sometimes add 8 ounces (226 g) of chicken drumsticks or whole chicken legs (including both the thigh and drumstick) while frying the vegetables. This gives the base so much flavor that there's no need to add any stock. She would then braise them with the soup, remove them and, once cool enough to handle, shred the meat and add it back into the soup.

As this is traditionally more of a vegetarian soup, I have used only vegetables, adding as much variety as possible. Any seasonal greens, such as a large savoy cabbage or a bunch of kale or spinach, work well to replace the Swiss chard. We add cannellini and borlotti (cranberry) beans to our minestrone, but if these are not available then 1 (14-ounce [400-g]) can of kidney or pinto beans will work nicely with the other vegetables. You can always double up on quantities if you can find only one type of beans.

The vegetables simmer for a few hours and develop so much flavor that there is really no need for any extra herbs, but that doesn't necessarily mean that you shouldn't add any. I keep it fairly simple with bay leaves, but you could use a handful of roughly chopped fresh parsley, thyme or basil leaves.

This recipe makes quite a large quantity of minestrone. You can divide it into containers and freeze it. It will keep in the freezer for up to 3 months, and all you would need to do is add some cooked pasta when you reheat it. Don't freeze your minestrone with cooked pasta in it. Over time the pasta will expand and will turn rubbery when reheated. It's always best to cook the pasta fresh and add it just before serving. Use 1 cup of cooked pasta per quart (liter) of soup. Make this minestrone your own by embracing what you have in your fridge and letting your imagination run wild.

(continued)

Hearty Minestrone (Continued)

→ **Makes 4.2 quarts (4 L), approximately 16 to 18 servings** ←

Ingredients

4 tbsp (60 ml) extra virgin olive oil

4 cloves garlic, peeled and finely chopped

1 white onion, diced

1 tbsp (16 g) tomato paste

1 (14-oz [400-g]) can diced tomatoes or 3 fresh tomatoes, diced

2 carrots, diced into 1-inch (2.5-cm) cubes

2 ribs celery, diced into 1-inch (2.5-cm) cubes

3 large potatoes, peeled and diced into 1-inch (2.5-cm) cubes

1 bunch Swiss chard, rinsed, stems removed and roughly chopped

⅓ cup (43 g) frozen peas

⅓ cup (45 g) frozen corn

4.2 quarts (4 L) water or just enough to cover the vegetables

2 vegetable stock cubes

2 bay leaves

Salt and freshly ground black pepper

Parmesan cheese rind (optional)

1 (14-oz [400-g]) can borlotti beans, drained

1 (14-oz [400-g]) can cannellini beans, drained

4 cups cooked pasta for serving (such as elbows, orzo, tiny shells or ditalini)

Shaved Parmesan cheese, for garnish

Method

In a large pot, add the olive oil over low-to-medium heat. Add the garlic and onion, and cook for 4 to 5 minutes, until the onion is translucent. If you want to use some protein, such as chicken legs or drumsticks, add it in the beginning. Fry it in a little olive oil until slightly browned. Remove it from the heat, put it into a bowl and add it back to the pot when you add the remaining vegetables. Add tomato paste and tomatoes and cook 1 to 2 minutes more to allow the tomato paste to cook off slightly and become fragrant.

Add the carrots, celery, potatoes, Swiss chard, peas and corn to the pot and stir to combine. Pour in enough water to cover the vegetables completely. Add the stock cubes (if you're not using any meat), bay leaves and season well with salt and pepper. Although not necessary, I love to add a Parmesan rind while the soup simmers for an extra flavor boost. Increase the heat slightly and bring to a gentle boil. Once the soup is boiling, reduce the heat to low, cover and simmer for up to 1½ hours, or until the vegetables are tender.

Add the borlotti and cannellini beans to the minestrone during the last 10 minutes of cooking. This is a large batch of soup, so I would recommend cooking the pasta separately according to the package instructions, or just until al dente if using my Egg Pasta Dough (page 32). Drain and add the cooked pasta to separate bowls.

Remove the bay leaves and Parmesan rind (if you are using it). Pour the minestrone soup over the pasta and serve it with lots of shaved Parmesan cheese on top accompanied by some fresh crunchy bread.

Divide the leftovers into airtight containers and put them in the freezer for a quick meal on another day.

Ziti al Forno

Al forno means "baked" and is a popular way of preparing this hearty pasta dish in Italian kitchens. Each region has its own unique way of adapting the recipe. For instance, in Sicily, they add boiled eggs to the baked dish, and in Campania they add vegetables such as eggplant and bell peppers. It's a very rustic pasta dish best served in the cooler months, and it tastes even better if you cook it in a wood-fire oven.

A versatile pasta bake, Ziti al Forno definitely paves the way to a creative dinner. Starting with the protein of the dish, ground beef is traditional, although using 12 ounces (340 g) of sausages, chicken or pork can be a lovely option. If you have made the Bolognese Sauce (page 16), then this would be a dream to add to the pasta bake, as it already has lots of flavor. If you use the Bolognese Sauce, do not use the ground beef listed here and replace the sugo di pomodoro with 2½ cups (600 ml) or more of the Bolognese Sauce.

I love to include boiled eggs, as it takes me back to the traditional Sunday lunch of my childhood, but feel free to leave them out. Baked ziti does not have any strict rules, so you can be as creative as you like. Dip a few slices of eggplant into some egg and bread crumbs, fry them in a little olive oil, slice them into strips and add them to the pasta mixture for a delicious vegetarian variation. I also like to add ½ cup (67 g) of frozen peas into the mix for some sweetness—not to mention a pop of color! You could even replace the tomato sauce with pesto sauce. As pesto has a stronger taste, be mindful of how much you're adding; I recommend using no more than 1½ cups (360 ml).

If you have some leftover hot salami, ham or prosciutto in the refrigerator, slice it up and add it. For an even quicker addition, try using 1 (15-ounce [425-g]) can of tuna in olive oil. Add it straight to the sauce just before combining all the ingredients. You may also like to add some broccoli florets, spinach or leafy greens such as kale or Tuscan cabbage. This dish can be made a day ahead. No matter which way you make Ziti al Forno, it's a hearty meal that the whole family will enjoy.

Ingredients

1 lb (454 g) dried ziti, penne or rigatoni pasta

2 tbsp (30 ml) extra virgin olive oil

2 cloves garlic, finely chopped

1 onion, finely chopped

1 tbsp (14 g) butter

12 oz (340 g) ground beef

Salt and freshly ground black pepper

2½ cups (600 ml) Mum's Homemade Sugo di Pomodoro (page 14)

½ cup (64 g) frozen peas

4 eggs, boiled and sliced

2 (7-oz [200-g]) mozzarella balls, roughly torn

1 cup (100 g) grated Parmesan cheese, plus more for serving

Method

Preheat the oven to 350°F (175°C). Bring a large pot of salted water to a boil and add the ziti or your choice of pasta. Cook just under the recommended cooking time, drain and set aside. If you would like to add some broccoli florets to this pasta bake, add them with the cooking pasta during last 5 minutes.

Heat the olive oil in a large saucepan over medium low heat. Add the garlic, onion and butter and cook for 2 to 3 minutes, until the onion is translucent and soft. Add the ground beef, or other protein, and season well with salt and pepper. Feel free to add your choice of extra herbs, such as oregano and thyme, or spices, such as 1 teaspoon of dried red pepper flakes.

Use a wooden spoon to break up the meat in the pan. Cook the ground beef for 5 to 7 minutes, or until browned and cooked through. Stir in Mum's Homemade Sugo di Pomodoro and add the frozen peas. Reduce the heat to low, cover and simmer for 10 minutes. Turn off

the heat, set aside and allow to cool slightly. If you're using my Bolognese Sauce (page 16) in this recipe, there will be no need for this cooking method, although you could add some extra herbs or spice to it.

To assemble, mix the cooked pasta into the sauce, and make sure all the pasta is coated. Add the sliced eggs and any other additions, such as salami or ham. Transfer to a large baking dish and nestle torn pieces of mozzarella into the bake. You could even use baby bocconcini, ricotta, provolone or burrata instead for a creamier flavor. Scatter grated Parmesan cheese all over the top.

Cover with foil and bake for 20 to 25 minutes. Remove the foil and bake for an extra 10 to 15 minutes, until the mozzarella has melted and the top layer starts to crisp and turn golden. Remove the dish from the oven and allow the pasta to rest for 10 to 15 minutes before serving.

Serve the Ziti al Forno with a generous amount of grated Parmesan cheese.

Ricotta Gnudi with Lemon Butter & Sage Sauce

With beautiful pillows of silky ricotta alongside a lemony buttery sage sauce, this Tuscan-inspired dish is in a class by itself. Gnudi or malfatti, as they are also known in Siena, are a special kind of "naked" pasta. *Malfatti* means "poorly made or done," because they are shaped by using your hands. They are similar to the filling of a ravioli without the casing, which is why they are sometimes called naked. Gnudi are lighter since fresh ricotta replaces potato as the main ingredient. I like to think of them as a large Italian dumpling that is packed full of flavor.

If fresh ricotta is unavailable to you, cottage cheese is definitely a viable option. Keep in mind that cottage cheese has a higher liquid content than ricotta cheese, so you will need to add more flour to make it easier to shape. I recommend adding an extra ¾ cup (94 g) of plain all-purpose flour and use 3 egg yolks instead of 2 whole eggs. I have added salty grated Parmesan cheese to these gnudi, but if you have some pecorino Romano or grana padano, you can use the same amount of 1½ cups (150 g) in the mixture. I recommend sticking to harder, grated cheeses if you decide to supplement the ricotta. They balance the ricotta and limit the amount of water. If you add a softer cheese such as mozzarella or burrata, you run the risk of the gnudi falling apart.

Gnudi can be cooked right after the dough is mixed, but I find that when you allow them to set in the refrigerator they retain their shape better. If you boil them immediately, little bits of dough may fall off, giving them a rough look. Allowing them to set for 2 hours in the fridge will help give them a smooth finish. If the mixture feels soft and wet, and you are unsure if they will hold their shape during the cooking process, you can try boiling one or two right away as a test. If they don't hold their shape, add a little more flour to the mixture, until you get the desired consistency. Once the gnudi rise to the surface of the boiling water and don't fall apart, you're good to go.

There are so many different herb flavor combinations that you can serve with homemade gnudi. Use 1 to 2 tablespoons (2 to 4 g) of your choice of hearty herbs—rosemary, oregano and thyme are wonderful and will easily replace the sage in this recipe. When you are using fresh herbs, pick the leaves off of the woody stems and give them a rough chop. This will release their natural fragrance and add a lot of flavor. If you prefer to keep the leaves intact, put the whole stem into the sauce.

Homemade gnudi are rustic and such a joy to make. These light pillows take a little time to create, but this is a dish that will keep everyone coming back for more.

Ingredients

14 oz (400 g) fresh ricotta cheese

2 whole eggs

½ cup (64 g) all-purpose flour, plus more for dusting

Pinch of ground nutmeg

1½ cups (150 g) grated Parmesan cheese, plus more for serving

Salt and freshly ground black pepper

5 tbsp (70 g) butter

20–25 fresh sage leaves, roughly torn

Zest and juice of 1 lemon

Method

To remove excess liquid from the ricotta, put it into a colander lined with a cheesecloth. For best results, drain the ricotta for at least 2 hours or overnight prior to cooking.

In a large bowl, add the drained ricotta, eggs, flour, grated nutmeg, Parmesan, salt and pepper, and mix well.

Fill a shallow bowl with the extra flour. Use a tablespoon to help form the balls, and then use your hands to finish rolling them into the desired shape. Gently place the gnudi into the flour to coat them. Put them onto a lined baking sheet, repeating until all the ricotta mixture has been used. Use a separate baking sheet if needed.

Put the gnudi into the refrigerator for 2 to 3 hours. This will help them to firm up and slightly dry out so they won't fall apart while cooking.

There are two ways you can cook the gnudi: Fry them in a little olive oil for 3 to 5 minutes on each side or until a golden layer is formed, or boil them in a pot of salted water. Once they rise to the surface, allow them to simmer for 2 to 3 more minutes before removing them from the water with a slotted spoon.

To prepare the lemon butter and sage sauce, add the butter to a saucepan over low heat to melt. Add the sage leaves and lemon zest, and season well with salt and pepper. Fry only for a few minutes, until the sage leaves turn crispy.

To serve, put the gnudi onto a plate, then spoon the lemon butter and sage sauce over the pasta and sprinkle with grated Parmesan and squeeze the lemon over top.

Orecchiette with Broccoli & Sausages

Throughout Italy orecchiette are traditionally served with broccoli rabe (*rapini*) or a simple chile and garlic sauce. My nonna makes orecchiette with broccoli and adds her own touch of 1 to 2 teaspoons (3 to 4 g) of paprika when frying the garlic. It gives the dish a mildly sweet flavor, as well as a rusty hue.

I have added a little chile to this dish, as I love the heat, although this is not necessary. Fennel seeds complement the pork sausage nicely. I recommend adding 1 to 2 teaspoons (2 to 4 g); any more than that can overpower the dish.

Pork sausage is used in this dish, although you can substitute ground beef or chicken. I recommend a similar amount of 14 ounces (400 g). If you want a healthier option, a great alternative would be 1 (14-ounce [400-g]) can of chickpeas or some sliced cherry tomatoes. Other complements: chopped Pepe Arrostiti (page 22) or 2¼ cups (120 g) of roughly chopped oil-packed sun-dried tomatoes, which can be added in with the broccoli.

I like to use baby broccoli in this dish, but feel free to use broccoli rabe if you prefer it. If you want to add another leafy green, 10.5 ounces (300 g) of baby spinach or kale would work just as well. I suggest adding any leafy greens in the last 2 to 3 minutes of cooking, as they wilt quickly, and you want them to retain as much flavor as possible.

Ingredients

14 oz (400 g) Italian pork sausage

2 bunches baby broccoli (also called broccolini)

¼ cup (60 ml) extra virgin olive oil

4 cloves garlic, finely sliced

2 tsp (4 g) mild paprika

1 medium fresh chile, seeded and finely chopped (optional)

1 lb (454 g) dried orecchiette or 1 batch Semolina Pasta Dough (page 25) formed into orecchiette (page 28)

½ cup (120 ml) reserved pasta water

½ cup (50 g) grated Parmesan cheese, plus more for serving

Salt and freshly ground black pepper

Method

Remove the sausage from their casings, break them up into smaller pieces with your hands and set aside. Rinse the baby broccoli, remove the woody ends and cut it into roughly ½-inch (1.3-cm) pieces. Alternatively, if baby broccoli is not available, 1 head of broccoli works perfectly. Trim off the stem and cut into small florets.

In a large saucepan, heat the olive oil over medium heat. Add the garlic and paprika and cook for 1 minute. Add the sausage meat to the saucepan, using a wooden spoon to break it apart. Add the fresh chile (if using), as well as your choice of any extra spices or herbs, such as a handful of fresh basil or some thyme leaves, and cook for 10 minutes, stirring occasionally to prevent the sausage from sticking to the bottom of the pan.

If you use ground beef or chicken, repeat the same steps above, making sure the meat is cooked through and browned. If you opt for canned chickpeas or another legume, drain the liquid completely and add the legumes to the saucepan after the cooked pasta and broccoli.

Bring a large pot of salted water to a boil and add the orecchiette. Cook for just under the recommended cooking time, or until al dente. Add the baby broccoli to the pasta for the last 5 minutes of cooking. If using homemade orecchiette, add the pasta first, then add the baby broccoli to the last 2 to 3 minutes of cooking. Reserve ½ cup (120 ml) of pasta water, drain the orecchiette and broccoli well and add them to the cooked sausage.

Pour the reserved pasta water into the pasta mixture, add the Parmesan, season with salt and pepper and stir until the sauce thickens and the pasta is well coated. Add in any leafy greens, if using.

Serve the orecchiette with extra Parmesan and a fresh chile, if desired.

Fettuccine Puttanesca

Originating in the seaside town of Naples in Campania, puttanesca is a thick and stunningly fragrant sauce. *Puttanesca* roughly translates as "lady of the night," which our imaginations interpret in many different ways! Puttanesca sauce is made up of simple ingredients, many of which can be found already in your kitchen. The saltiness of the capers and anchovies mixed with Kalamata olives brings this dish—and your taste buds—to life.

Tuna in olive oil (1 [15-ounce (425-g)] can) or a piece of cooked salmon make excellent additions to this sauce. I suggest cooking the salmon separately, tearing it into flakes and popping it into the sauce just before adding the pasta. Roasted red peppers are another lovely alternative to enhance the flavor of the dish and give it a vegetarian twist—use 3.5 ounces (100 g) of Pepe Arrostiti (page 22). Traditionally, you would use black pitted olives, but I use a mix of black and green olives, as I love the flavor of both of them combined. Feel free to use what you have on hand, just remember to make sure your olives are pitted.

Capers are a wonderful addition if you are not a fan of fish. They are salty enough, but if they are not your cup of tea, you can always use extra olives. There is no added salt in this recipe, as the anchovies and capers are already quite salty on their own. If you decide not to use these, please remember to season the sauce well with salt. Leafy greens such as Swiss chard or kale, around 7 ounces (200 g), are another excellent addition.

Fettuccine Puttanesca is one of my favorite dishes to make, as it was one of the very first meals I used to cook when I moved out of my childhood home. I love to serve the sauce on its own with slices of ciabatta on the side. It is definitely my standard Friday night dinner.

Ingredients

¼ cup (60 ml) extra virgin olive oil

4 cloves garlic, finely chopped

1 shallot, finely chopped

10 whole anchovy fillets in olive oil, drained

2 (14-oz [400-g]) cans diced tomatoes

2 tbsp (30 g) baby capers, drained

3.5 oz (100 g) mixed pitted green and black olives, roughly chopped

1 tsp dried red pepper flakes, plus more for serving (optional)

1 lb (454 g) dried fettuccine or 1 batch Egg Pasta Dough (page 32), rolled and cut into fettuccine (page 35)

3 tbsp (11 g) finely chopped fresh flat-leaf parsley

Method

Bring a large pot of water to a boil. While it's coming to a boil, in a large saucepan heat the olive oil over medium heat. Add the garlic and shallot and cook for 2 to 3 minutes, until the shallot softens, stirring occasionally. Add the anchovies to the pan, gently stirring until they start to fall apart.

Pour in the tomatoes, capers, olives and red pepper flakes (if using), and stir to combine. If you are adding some canned tuna in olive oil to the sauce, make sure you drain as much of the oil as possible prior to adding it to the pan, as it may cause the sauce to be too oily. Reduce the heat to low, cover and simmer for 10 to 15 minutes to allow the sauce to thicken and become fragrant.

Add salt to the water for the pasta once it has come to a boil, then add the fettuccine, making sure the pasta is completely submerged. Cook the fettuccine just under the recommended cooking time, drain and add straight into the simmering sauce. If you want to make homemade fettucine for this dish, make the dough and pasta before you make the sauce. There will be enough time for the pasta to rest and cook while the sauce is simmering.

Toss the fettuccine gently with the sauce, making sure the pasta is well coated. If you would like to add any fresh leafy greens such as baby spinach or kale, put them in right at the end, as they will wilt with the residual heat.

Serve the Fettuccine Puttanesca in bowls or on a large platter with parsley and extra red pepper flakes, if desired.

Gnocchi alla Romana

This is comfort food at its best. Roman gnocchi are made a little bit differently than traditional potato gnocchi. The main ingredient is semolina flour, which is much finer and lighter in texture and creates light fluffy pillows of heaven. What is not to love about that? Semolina is a type of durum wheat that is used in pasta making and helps the gnocchi keep its structure and shape when cooking. The semolina rounds are overlapped in a buttered baking dish, topped with melted butter and lots of grated Parmesan cheese and baked until golden.

All-purpose or bread flour is a great alternative if semolina is not available. Polenta (cornmeal) can also fill in for the semolina. It's a wonderful gluten-free option, and you can use gluten-free bread crumbs on the top. Since polenta is made from corn, it will have a different taste when combined with the other ingredients. You could also try using both polenta and semolina, adding 4 ounces (113 g) of each for a different twist.

Skim milk can be used as an alternative to whole milk. Chicken stock may also be substituted for the milk for a version that's lower in fat. Or, for a more intense, richer version of the dish, try adding 2.5 ounces (71 g) of Gorgonzola cheese. You can also serve this type of gnocchi with my Mum's Homemade Sugo di Pomodoro (page 14).

You can prepare this dish ahead of time, store it in the refrigerator and pop it in the oven when you're ready to eat. Gnocchi alla Romana are so easy to make that you can get the whole family involved in the kitchen.

→ **Makes 6 to 8 servings** ←

Ingredients

3 cups (720 ml) whole milk

1½ cups (250 g) fine-ground semolina flour

½ tsp ground nutmeg

1 tsp salt

2 egg yolks, beaten

3½ tbsp (50 ml) melted butter, divided, plus more for the baking dish

1½ cups (150 g) grated Parmesan cheese, divided

¼ cup (27 g) dried bread crumbs

Method

In a medium sauccpan, warm the milk over low heat for 2 to 3 minutes. Once the milk is warm, slowly whisk in the semolina and the nutmeg. Continue to whisk until it reaches a smooth consistency. Cook over very low heat for about 8 to 10 minutes. As the mixture begins to thicken, you will notice that it will start to pull away from the sides. Once that begins to happen, switch over to a wooden spoon and stir continuously. The mixture will turn into a thick dough-like consistency, which becomes tougher to work with but is exactly what you're after. Turn off the heat, and set the dough aside to cool to room temperature.

Once the dough has cooled, add the salt, egg yolks, half of the butter and 1 cup (100 g) of the Parmesan cheese and stir until well incorporated. Line a 12 x 18–inch (30 x 45–cm) baking sheet with parchment paper and pour the contents evenly over the paper, roughly ¼ inch (6 mm) in height. Use a rubber spatula or knife to spread it into an even layer. Cover with plastic wrap and put into the fridge for 2 to 3 hours, until firm.

When the dough is set, preheat the oven to 350°F (175°C), and grease a 1-quart (900-ml) oval baking dish with a little butter. Remove the dough from the fridge and with a 1½- to 2-inch (4- to 5-cm) cookie cutter or a drinking glass, cut the dough into circular shapes. Layer them onto the base of the baking dish, overlapping each other. Repeat the process until the entire base of the baking dish is covered.

Dot the top with the remaining butter and scatter the remaining Parmesan cheese all over. If you wish, crumble a creamy blue cheese such as Gorgonzola over the top of the gnocchi for a really deep flavor. Sprinkle the bread crumbs on top, put the dish into the oven and bake for 25 to 30 minutes, until the cheese is bubbling and golden brown.

To serve with homemade sauce, heat 1 to 2 cups (240 to 480 ml) of Mum's Homemade Sugo di Pomodoro (page 14) in a saucepan, until warm. Spread a layer of sauce on each plate and put the gnocchi on the top of the sauce.

Serve the Gnocchi alla Romana alongside a fresh garden salad.

Classic Spaghetti Carbonara

I spent a little time in Rome a while back, and I ate the most beautiful plate of pasta carbonara. It was silky and glorious with shaved pieces of black truffle scattered all around the plate. I fell in love immediately. The Romans sure know how to put on a show with their signature pasta dish, using the simplest of ingredients in the most brilliant way.

Traditional carbonara is made with fresh eggs, guanciale (cured pork cheek), pecorino Romano cheese and black pepper. I cannot stress this enough: A classic carbonara uses raw eggs and without them, it's not really a carbonara. The eggs are the hero of the dish and when mixed with the starchy pasta water they create a wonderful silky, creamy sauce that coats and complements the pasta. Because there are so few ingredients, you want to make sure the ones you use are fresh and of good quality.

When it comes to the pork, I use either guanciale or pancetta. The main reason for using these is that they both have a high fat content, which creates a good base for the carbonara. Guanciale is cured, salty and has a high fat-to-meat ratio. Because guanciale is not as readily available around the world, pancetta is something that I tend to use quite often and is the next best alternative. From the belly of the pig, it has more meat than guanciale, but it also has a high fat content, so when it cooks, the fat renders and creates a crispy meat, and there's no need to add any oil.

If neither of these options is available, then bacon would be best. Keep in mind that the smoked flavor and any spices will change the taste of your dish, giving you a completely different experience. A nontraditional approach would be to add 13 ounces (390 g) of baby spinach or kale to replace the meat, but doing so will change the taste of the dish entirely. If you use spinach or kale, cook it down in a little olive oil to create the base of your sauce. You could also add 2 medium-sized zucchini, diced and cooked in a little olive oil, until soft and slightly golden. For an earthier flavor addition, sauté 1½ cups (105 g) of white mushrooms in a little olive oil or butter until they are golden brown on both sides. Remove the mushrooms from the heat and add them to the cream sauce toward the end of the cooking time.

Pecorino Romano is commonly used, as it has a sharp, salty, bold taste, where Parmesan has a milder, nuttier flavor. I've used both cheeses separately as well as combined, and they both work. Using ¾ cup (75 g) each of pecorino and Parmesan will provide a nutty, savory flavor. Carbonara loves black pepper, as it complements the dish perfectly and adds a spicy kick. The cured pork and cheeses are salty enough, so there is no reason for additional salt. A fresh herb such as parsley is both aromatic and visually bright. This creamy carbonara is the perfect sauce for thick-shaped pasta and pairs well with homemade fettucine (page 35). My carbonara recipe is foolproof and delicious and will take you no time at all to whip up for a midweek Roman feast.

Makes 6 servings

Ingredients

3 eggs, beaten

1 cup (100 g) Pecorino Romano cheese, finely grated, plus more for serving

½ cup (50 g) Parmesan cheese, finely grated, plus more for serving

Lots of freshly ground black pepper

10.5 oz (300 g) pancetta or guanciale, diced into small pieces

1 lb (454 g) dried spaghetti

1 cup (240 ml) reserved pasta water

Method

Prepare the ingredients for the sauce by adding the eggs, cheeses and ground pepper into a bowl and whisking until combined. Set aside.

In a medium-sized saucepan, add the diced pancetta or guanciale, and cook over low heat until the fat starts to render and the meat turns crispy, about 5 to 6 minutes. If you are using bacon, the thickness will determine the length of time it takes to cook. Keep an eye on it, but it should take about 3 to 5 minutes on each side to cook until crispy. If replacing the pancetta with baby spinach, cook with a little olive oil over low heat for about 2 to 3 minutes, until wilted.

While the pancetta is cooking, fill a pot with water and bring it to a boil. Salt the water and add the spaghetti. Cook the pasta just under the recommended time, as it will continue to cook once you combine all the ingredients together. Reserve 1 cup (240 ml) of pasta water and set it aside, then drain the pasta and add it to the pancetta. Gently toss the spaghetti with the pancetta and add in some of the reserved pasta water, a little at a time, as this helps deglaze the bottom of the saucepan.

This is very important: You must remove the saucepan from the heat before adding the egg mixture. When eggs hit a very hot pan they immediately start to scramble, which is something you do not want. Pull the saucepan away from the heat and allow it to cool for 1 or 2 minutes prior to adding the eggs. This will allow the mixture to keep its silky consistency and not curdle.

Pour in the egg mixture a little at a time, while continually stirring the pasta. The residual heat will cook the eggs and create a creamy sauce. Once all of the egg mixture has been incorporated into the pasta, keep on stirring it to reach the desired silky consistency. You can always add extra grated cheese if you feel your sauce is a little runny (in my eyes, adding more cheese is not really a bad thing). The spaghetti should be evenly coated in the silky sauce.

Serve on a platter with another scattering of grated cheese and more freshly ground pepper.

Pasta Perfetto ➔ 65

Rigatoni alla Vodka

One of the newer sauces, alla vodka was created in Italy during the 1980s and has become a popular addition to many restaurants around the country and worldwide. I've made the traditional penne alla vodka many times, and it's always a hit. It is a classic combination with a hint of vodka to tantalize your taste buds. In this recipe I've used rigatoni, the grooves of which capture all that delicious, thick sauce.

Adding vodka to this sauce alters the flavor in a pleasing way. The combination of heavy cream and vodka creates a rich and creamy element that mellows the acidity in the sauce. Using the best-quality vodka you can get your hands on will really elevate the taste. Try 3.5 ounces (100 g) of ricotta instead of the cream for a healthier alternative.

This recipe calls for whole canned tomatoes, which allow you to make it at any time of year. If tomatoes are in season, whole plum tomatoes are a wonderful alternative—about 6 to 8 is a good amount. To remove the skins from the fresh plum tomatoes, core the top of the tomatoes and put them into a boiling pot of water for about 20 seconds. Once cool enough to handle, the skin should be easy to peel off. You could also add 2 cups (480 ml) of my Mum's Homemade Sugo di Pomodoro (page 14) if you want a smoother sauce.

The sauce relies on a very few simple ingredients, and the addition of leafy greens, such as spinach, kale or Tuscan cabbage, would provide a pop of color. You could quite easily turn this dish into a white sauce by omitting the tomatoes and the tomato paste and using mushrooms. Sauté the mushrooms in batches over low heat in a little butter for 2 to 3 minutes, until they're brown and crispy.

Fresh herbs such as torn basil leaves will add a lovely sweet freshness to the dish, or for that extra heat, add some dried red pepper flakes. Homemade orecchiette (page 28) or cavatelli (page 30) using 1 batch of Semolina Pasta Dough (page 25) are great substitutes for the rigatoni if you wish.

Ingredients

2 (14-oz [400-g]) cans whole tomatoes

2 tbsp (30 ml) extra virgin olive oil

3 cloves garlic, peeled and finely chopped

1 shallot, finely chopped

2 tbsp (32 g) tomato paste

2.5 oz (74 ml) good-quality vodka

½ cup (120 ml) heavy cream

1–2 tsp (2–4 g) dried red pepper flakes or dried oregano (optional)

1 lb (454 g) dried rigatoni pasta

Salt and freshly ground black pepper

½ cup (50 g) grated Parmesan cheese, plus more for serving

A handful of fresh basil leaves, roughly torn

Method

Use your hands to crush the tomatoes into a bowl. Reserve the remaining liquid from the can for another use—such as when you're making a quick pasta sauce or a minestrone soup base. If you opt for fresh plum tomatoes, after you remove the skins, dice them into pieces and set aside. In a large saucepan, heat the olive oil over low heat. Add the garlic and shallot and cook for 2 to 3 minutes, until the shallot is soft and translucent.

Stir in the tomato paste and cook for a few minutes before adding the tomatoes. The tomato paste will intensify the flavor and create a rich, bold sauce. Add the tomatoes and increase the heat to medium. Carefully pour in the vodka and cook off the alcohol completely, roughly 5 minutes.

Pour in the heavy cream (or ricotta, if using) and mix well. Add the herbs and spices of your choice, including dried red pepper flakes or dried oregano. Reduce the heat to low, and simmer the sauce for 8 to 10 minutes to allow all those flavors to combine and the sauce to thicken.

Meanwhile, fill a large pot with water and bring to a boil. Add some salt to the water, then add the rigatoni. Cook for just under the recommended cooking time. Drain the pasta and add it to the simmering sauce. Season well with salt and pepper, and toss in the Parmesan right at the very end.

Serve the Rigatoni alla Vodka with extra grated Parmesan cheese and torn basil.

Classic Homemade Lasagna

Homemade lasagna is, in my opinion, the ultimate comfort food. The cheesy, saucy goodness creates a wonderfully satisfying feeling, from each delicious mouthful to mopping up the sauce with a piece of bread at the very end. My favorite part of lasagna is the crunchy outer edges. When my family makes it, I always put my hand up for those crunchy corners.

Remember making that beautiful Bolognese Sauce (page 16)? I would highly recommend using it for this lasagna recipe. With so much flavor packed into the sauce from the get-go, it's an ideal starting point for any great lasagna. Of course, you can opt to make a simple ragu with 1 pound (454 g) of ground beef, pork or lamb with chopped garlic, onion, diced carrots, diced celery and tomato puree. If you prefer, you can stick to my Mum's Homemade Sugo di Pomodoro (page 14).

Lasagna is traditionally made with ground beef ragu and a silky béchamel sauce, then it's covered in cheese and baked until golden brown. Over the years it has been widely altered to suit many different styles and taste buds, so changing the style of a traditional lasagna is welcomed. Try a vegetarian version, using roasted vegetables such as 2 large eggplants (sliced), 1 large pumpkin (peeled and sliced) or 2 large zucchini. Drizzle the veggies with extra virgin olive oil and roast them in a preheated 350°F (175°C) oven for 15 to 20 minutes, until soft. You could also brown 2 cups of sliced mushrooms with 1 bunch of leafy greens such as kale, spinach or Swiss chard. Or use my Vegetarian Sauce (page 18).

Instead of the Parmesan, add the same amount of grated Gruyère or shredded mozzarella or fontina. Adding a few dots of ricotta in between the lasagna layers is also a brilliant option. I like to keep the seasoning fairly simple with this béchamel sauce because it already has so much going on in the taste department. However, if you would

like to give it a little boost of herbs, I suggest a bay leaf, a pinch of fresh thyme or some finely chopped parsley. If you use a bay leaf in the béchamel, remember to remove it prior to spreading the sauce.

You can use dried or fresh lasagna sheets for this recipe, but I urge you to make my Egg Pasta Dough (page 32). Roll out the dough according to the instructions, on the thinnest setting, and cut it into sheets to cover your baking dish. Making the lasagna a day in advance will allow all the flavors to combine. Never underestimate the power of a homemade lasagna—it is such a wonderfully rich, comforting and satisfying meal.

Ingredients

1½ cups (150 g) grated Parmesan cheese, plus more for serving

1½ cups (170 g) shredded mozzarella cheese

5–6 cups (1.2–1.4 L) Bolognese Sauce (page 16), Vegetarian Sauce (page 18) or
Mum's Homemade Sugo di Pomodoro (page 14)

1 batch Egg Pasta Dough (page 32), rolled and cut into lasagna sheets, or 16 dried lasagna sheets

Béchamel Sauce

2 tbsp (30 g) butter

⅔ cup (80 g) all-purpose flour

2 cups (480 ml) whole milk

¼ tsp ground nutmeg

Salt and freshly ground black pepper

½ cup (50 g) grated Parmesan cheese

Method

If you are adding a vegetarian twist to this lasagna, prepare the vegetables any way you prefer: grilled, baked or fried.

Mix the Parmesan and mozzarella together in a bowl and set aside.

To make the béchamel sauce: Heat a saucepan over medium heat, melt the butter and whisk in the flour until smooth. Slowly pour in the milk while continuing to whisk to prevent any lumps. Reduce the heat to low, and add the ground nutmeg and salt and pepper, then simmer for 5 minutes to thicken. Once cooked, remove it from the heat and add the grated Parmesan and whisk until smooth and silky. Set aside to cool slightly. Preheat the oven to 350°F (175°C).

To assemble the lasagna, I find that it's not necessary to boil the pasta sheets before baking, especially when using fresh pasta, as long as there is enough liquid in the sauces. If you prefer, follow the instructions on the package to parboil them. Avoid cooking them until tender as they will then become mushy in the oven.

In a 10 x 10–inch (25 x 25–cm) deep casserole dish, spread a little of whichever sauce you're using over the base of your baking dish. Add a layer of lasagna sheets, then pour a layer of sauce over the lasagna sheets, making sure they are covered. If you are adding roasted vegetables, layer these evenly over the pasta. Pour a ladle or two of béchamel over the sauce or vegetables, then add a light layer of the mixed cheeses.

Repeat with another layer of pasta sheets, followed by sauce (and vegetables, if using), béchamel and mixed cheeses. A lasagna should have a minimum of three layers, so work your way until you reach about four or even five layers, if your casserole dish allows. Never overfill your lasagna, as you run the risk of it spilling over in the oven.

Top off the lasagna with a final layer of sauce and the remaining cheeses. Cover with aluminum foil and bake for 40 minutes. Remove the foil and bake for another 10 minutes, until the top is golden brown and the cheese is bubbling. Allow to sit for 10 to 15 minutes before cutting. Serve with a little more grated Parmesan.

Chapter Three

The Great Pizza Journey

➤ ⟵

Pizza—the holy grail of Italian food. Throughout the streets of Italy, you are graced with delicious pizza rustica on every corner. Wrapped in brown paper and served hot, this fast food is widely popular in its own right, which is why I have dedicated a whole chapter to it. If you have been lucky enough to live in or visit this beautiful country, you might have found that one place that serves the pizza that tantalized your taste buds in every way possible. Your mouth is watering right now, isn't it?

My family's homemade pizza is always made with so much love and care. My nonna would make her traditional Margherita pizza (page 72) with homemade dough, which rested for hours before it was shaped. She covered it in a light tomato sauce and sprinkled fragrant grated Parmesan cheese on top. Before it even hit the dinner table, the entire tray would be devoured. I wanted to pay homage to my family's Homemade Pizza Dough (page 38), as it has been my absolute favorite for years. This is more of a traditional Southern style of Margherita pizza, in which the dough is thicker.

Slow down time to enjoy the process of making pizza with your family. The classic flavor combos in this section are easy to adapt, and by trusting your intuition and using your own preferred toppings, you can make your own standout homemade pizza for the whole family to enjoy. Venturing into other shapes, use the Homemade Pizza Dough (page 38) as the base for Swiss Chard & Mushroom Calzones (page 84), which can be filled with so many glorious flavor combinations, including salty salami and mozzarella or perhaps even a sweet alternative such as Nutella and crushed walnuts.

Whether you experiment with different tastes or keep it simple with the classics, making pizza is a great way for family members to connect and be creative in the kitchen.

Classic Margherita Pizza

How can you go wrong with the classic Margherita pizza? It was created in Naples by the 19th-century chef Raffaele Esposito in honor of Queen Margherita of Savoy.

Because it's such a simple pizza, it's challenging to substitute ingredients. Instead, focus on mastering the elements of the dough and the sauce. If you're lucky enough to have made my Mum's Homemade Sugo di Pomodoro (page 14) and have some saved in your freezer, you already have the perfect go-to sauce for the base of your Margherita pizza. It has so much flavor already that you don't need much to add to the sauce. Of course, you can most definitely add some extras to elevate the sauce even further. Add 1 to 2 teaspoons (2 to 4 g) of dried red pepper flakes or a fresh red chile for extra heat or 2 or 3 anchovy fillets for their saltiness. Instead of using sauce you can substitute 1 (14-ounce [400-g]) can of diced tomatoes or 2 or 3 cups (300 or 450 g) of cherry tomatoes cooked down with a little olive oil, a few cloves of sliced garlic and salt and pepper.

Cheese is another very important ingredient. You want to stick to cheese that tastes delicious and can retain its shape during baking. Mozzarella, of course, is the best cheese for pizza. It's super creamy, decadent and looks incredible once melted. You can also use fresh bocconcini or burrata for an even creamier taste.

My nonna takes a different approach to her home-style pizza. She adds 1 cup (100 g) or more of grated Parmesan cheese on top of her Margherita pizza, which gives it some sharpness. This method of hers was adopted during her childhood, when the family had access to very few ingredients. Back then they didn't have fresh mozzarella at their disposal, so grated Parmesan cheese or pecorino was the next best thing. Feel free to use 1 cup (100 g) of grated pecorino Romano cheese for a slightly aged, nutty and salty flavor. Though this recipe uses torn pieces of fresh mozzarella, I encourage you to try my nonna's Parmesan variation when you're in the mood to switch things up or crave pizza but have no fresh mozzarella on hand.

Adding some fresh basil leaves just before serving is a must for this classic pizza. I am a firm believer in using it; there is nothing else quite like it. You can add whole leaves or finely slice or roughly tear them. I don't recommend adding fresh basil leaves prior to baking, as the heat will cause them to shrivel up and lose their flavor, not to mention their gorgeous green hue! Of course, dried herbs such as basil and oregano could be substituted or even added along with the fresh. This can be done either prior to or after baking and is equally delicious.

Makes 1 large pizza

Ingredients

1 batch Homemade Pizza Dough (page 38)

2 tbsp (30 ml) extra virgin olive oil, plus more for drizzling

1½ cups (360 ml) Mum's Homemade Sugo di Pomodoro (page 14)

Salt and freshly ground black pepper

9 oz (250 g) fresh mozzarella, torn

A handful of fresh basil leaves, torn

Method

Make the Homemade Pizza Dough.

Lightly coat a 12 x 18–inch (30 x 45–cm) baking sheet with the olive oil and stretch out the dough to cover the base of the sheet.

Preheat the oven to 400°F (200°C). Spread the sauce or diced tomatoes over the dough.

After adding the sauce to the pizza dough, drizzle a generous amount of extra virgin olive oil over the top and season with a little salt and pepper. If you substitute dried basil for the fresh basil, add up to 1 tablespoon (5 g) of dried basil at this point.

Put the pizza in the oven and bake it for 20 to 25 minutes. Remove the pizza from the oven and add the torn mozzarella, or your cheese of choice. Put the pizza back into the oven and bake for 10 more minutes, or until all the cheese has melted.

Remove from the oven, and then scatter the fresh basil leaves over the pizza and slice.

Spicy 'Nduja Pizza

'Nduja (pronounced en-DOO-ya) is a perfectly spiced spreadable salami that originates from the region of Calabria, in southern Italy. Typically made from various parts of the pig, such as the shoulder or belly, 'nduja is mainly composed of fat with some lean meat. With the combination of the fiery heat of authentic Calabrian chiles, it is a perfect addition to pizza!

It is a versatile ingredient and can be used in a variety of dishes. It can be added to pasta sauces or it can be spread over slices of fresh ciabatta. Its high fat content allows it to remain soft even after curing, and it can be eaten cooked or as is.

Hot sopressata salami can be used as a substitute and offers the same amount of heat. If you want to keep the taste fairly mild, cacciatore salami can be used to add a salty element to the pizza without the heat. Use a similar amount—3.5 ounces (100 g) or more—of sopressata or cacciatore if you cannot get your hands on this delicious spreadable salami. Sliced chorizo sausage, with its smoky, salty taste also works, but you can use whichever salami you like best.

Mozzarella or burrata is perfect for this pizza, and I suggest adding it during the last 10 minutes of baking, just so it melts through. You can also use bocconcini halves, or if you want a creamier texture, add a few dollops of ricotta or crumbles of feta.

In this recipe, I've added the 'nduja to my Mum's Homemade Sugo di Pomodoro (page 14) so it can be easily spread over the base of the pizza. If you are using a sliced salami, sopressata or chorizo, spread the sauce

over the base first and then layer the slices on top. If you do not have any of the Mum's Homemade Sugo di Pomodoro on hand, use 1½ cups (360 ml) of tomato puree, seasoned with salt and pepper.

Add as much or as little 'nduja as you like. It is a brilliant addition to your pizza—but only if you can stand the heat!

Ingredients

1 batch Homemade Pizza Dough (page 38)

2 tbsp (30 ml) extra virgin olive oil

1½ cups (360 ml) Mum's Homemade Sugo di Pomodoro (page 14) or tomato puree

3.5 oz (100 g) 'nduja or any other salami, such as sopressata (hot) or cacciatore (mild)

4 oz (125 g) fresh mozzarella, torn

½ cup (50 g) grated Parmesan cheese

1 tsp dried red pepper flakes (optional)

Method

Make the Homemade Pizza Dough.

Lightly coat a 12 x 18–inch (30 x 45 cm) baking sheet with the olive oil and stretch out the dough to cover the base of the sheet.

Preheat the oven to 400°F (200°C). If you prefer a chunky fresh sauce, take a look at my Classic Margherita Pizza recipe (page 72) for a fresh, quick and simple sauce. Alternatively, 1½ cups (360 ml) of tomato puree, seasoned with salt and pepper will work just as well for the base of the pizza.

You can prepare the 'nduja for the pizza in two different ways: Add the homemade sauce to the base of the pizza and spread the 'nduja on top. Or you can heat the homemade sauce in a small saucepan, add the 'nduja and cook for 4 to 5 minutes. This will allow the meat to melt evenly into the sauce. Once cooked, pour the sauce onto the base of the pizza. If you're using sliced salami, layer it evenly over the sauce.

Put the pizza in the oven and bake for 20 to 25 minutes. Take the pizza out of the oven and scatter the torn mozzarella evenly over it. Repeat with the Parmesan. Put the pizza back into the oven and bake for 10 more minutes, or until the cheese has melted.

Serve your Spicy 'Nduja Pizza topped with dried red pepper flakes, if desired, for an extra bit of heat.

Quattro Formaggi Pizza

This pizza is for all the cheese lovers out there! Pizza bianca or white pizza is made with four cheeses: mozzarella, Parmesan, Gorgonzola and fontina. Each is very different from the other and when combined, they taste absolutely fantastic. The cheeses can be altered to suit your taste. The key to a really great pizza bianca is to select the right types of cheeses and use the best-quality ingredients you can find.

Pizza bianca is made without the traditional tomato base used in a Margherita pizza. It relies on drizzled olive oil and salt with a layer of creamy cheeses all over the base to bring it to life.

For the base, you want to start off with a creamy cheese such as shredded mozzarella. I love to use fresh mozzarella because of its mild, salty flavor. It's also perfect for pizza because it melts really well without becoming watery. Feel free to substitute ½ cup (125 g) of fresh ricotta. It has a creamy, sweet, mild taste, and it can be easily spread over the base of the pizza.

Fontina is similar to mozzarella in that it also melts well, but it has a woody, tangy flavor. Fontina is readily available at most grocery stores, although if you're unable to find it, you can use 2 ounces (60 g) of Gruyère, provolone or Gouda.

Gorgonzola is a very strong, fragrant and creamy blue cheese that, depending on its age, adds a very sharp flavor. Since it's such a strong, rich cheese, I tend to use only a little, as it can be overpowering, but feel free to use as much as you like. If you are not into these strong types of

cheeses, use 1 ounce (30 g) of crumbled feta or goat cheese, which also adds tangy boldness without hijacking the flavor profile.

I like to finish the pizza off with either Parmesan or pecorino Romano. They both offer a complementary sharp, salty or nutty taste.

→ **Makes 1 large pizza** ←

Ingredients

1 batch Homemade Pizza Dough (page 38)

2 tbsp (30 ml) extra virgin olive oil, plus more for the pan

1 clove garlic, minced

2.5 oz (70 g) fresh mozzarella, drained and torn

¼ cup (60 g) grated fontina

1 oz (30 g) Gorgonzola, crumbled

½ cup (50 g) grated Parmesan

A handful of fresh sage leaves

Method

Make the Homemade Pizza Dough.

Lightly coat a 12 x 18–inch (30 x 45–cm) baking sheet with olive oil and stretch out the dough to cover the base of the sheet.

Preheat the oven to 400°F (200°C). In a small bowl, mix the olive oil and garlic together. Use a tablespoon or a brush to lightly cover the base of the pizza with the mixture. If you want to add a little coat of sauce to the base, evenly spread 4 to 5 tablespoons (60 to 75 ml) of homemade tomato sauce, tomato puree or pesto over the base. Just remember to keep it light!

Layer the mozzarella evenly over the base followed by fontina. Add the Gorgonzola then scatter the Parmesan all over the top. Add the fresh sage leaves or, if you prefer, thyme or oregano leaves.

Put the pizza in the oven and bake for 20 to 25 minutes, until the cheese has melted and turned golden.

Caramelized Onion & Mushroom Pizza

Mushrooms are incredibly versatile, and they are used in an array of dishes throughout many cultures.
I like to use a different variety of mushrooms when it comes to this particular pizza. The contrasting colors, as well as the texture and flavors, are stunning.

I like to sauté my mushrooms in batches with a little olive oil or butter prior to adding them to my pizza. This helps reduce some of the water content in them and gives them a golden texture and buttery taste. White button and portobello mushrooms have a nutty flavor that complements the caramelized onions extremely well. You can also substitute porcini, oyster or shiitake mushrooms. These all have a very earthy taste and are quite meaty, so they make a hearty addition to homemade pizzas.

The onions break down in the heat, caramelizing, and they are perfect additions to pizza and pasta dishes. Adding some brown sugar or 1 to 2 tablespoons (15 to 30 ml) of balsamic vinegar creates a sticky texture when cooked down, which tastes absolutely delicious. If you want to add some other vegetables, try a few sliced marinated artichoke hearts.

Fresh or dried herbs such as rosemary and thyme are great for this type of pizza. They both have earthy flavors, and they make a good duo. We all know that truffle oil and mushrooms complement each other well. If you're able to get your hands on some truffle oil or, better yet, freshly grated black truffle, adding it to this pizza would be a wonderful way to elevate this dish.

Pizza

1 batch Homemade Pizza Dough (page 38)

2 tbsp (30 ml) extra virgin olive oil, plus more for the pizza base

2 cups (140 g) mixed white button, portobello or cremini mushrooms, sliced

1 clove garlic, minced

½ tsp fresh or dried rosemary leaves

½ tsp fresh or dried thyme leaves

1 tsp dried red pepper flakes (optional)

4 oz (125 g) fresh burrata cheese

Caramelized Onions

2 white onions, peeled and sliced

2 tbsp (30 ml) extra virgin olive oil

2 tbsp (30 g) butter

¼ cup (55 g) brown sugar or 1–2 tbsp (15–30 ml) balsamic vinegar (optional)

Salt

Method

Make the Homemade Pizza Dough.

Lightly coat a 12 x 18–inch (30 x 45–cm) baking sheet with olive oil and stretch out the dough to cover the base of the tray.

To make the caramelized onions: Put the sliced onions into a small saucepan over low heat. Add the olive oil and butter and stir to combine. Cook over very low heat for about 30 minutes, stirring occasionally to prevent them from sticking to the bottom of the saucepan. Add a tablespoon or two (15 or 30 ml) of water from time to time if they begin to stick. Add in either the brown sugar or balsamic vinegar, if using, stir and simmer until the sugar has dissolved and the onions take on a sticky texture. Once cooked, remove from the heat, add some salt and set aside.

As mentioned, I love to sauté my mushrooms prior to adding them to my pizza. You can add them straight onto your pizza if you like, but if you want to cook them, begin by heating a saucepan and adding the 2 tablespoons (30 ml) of olive oil. Working in batches, cook the mushrooms for 2 to 3 minutes, until they are slightly golden in color. Transfer them to a bowl and set aside. Mushrooms have a high water content, so before you add them to the pizza, remember to drain the liquid thoroughly.

Preheat the oven to 400°F (200°C). Cover the base of the pizza dough with a little olive oil and the minced garlic. For a salty twist, you could use the anchovy and rosemary–infused oil from my Anchovy & Rosemary Oil Focaccia with Olives recipe (page 122). (It already has olive oil and garlic, so there's no need to add the garlic and oil from this recipe.) Scatter the caramelized onions evenly over the pizza base and add the mixed mushrooms. Season with rosemary and thyme or your choice of fresh or dried herbs. As always, I love to add some heat with dried red pepper flakes, so sprinkle them on if using.

Put the pizza in the oven and bake for 20 to 25 minutes. Remove the pizza from the oven and add the torn burrata (or other cheese of your choice) over the top. Put the pizza back into the oven and bake for 10 more minutes, or until the cheese has melted.

Remove the pizza from the oven, slice and serve. If desired, drizzle some truffle oil onto the pizza for an extra earthy flavor.

Grilled Vegetable Pizza

When it comes to vegetable pizza, there are no rules about toppings. You can be as creative as you want and use whatever ingredients you have on hand.

When working with vegetables, it's always best to stick to ones that are in season. During the cooler months ingredients such as sweet potatoes and pumpkin are great options, where bell peppers, eggplant, summer squash and zucchini are best in the warmer months. Of course, many may be available regardless of the season, but can be quite costly.

Using the freshest ingredients available to you is always best when making pizzas. I love to cook my own vegetables with a little olive oil in a grill pan, but to save time you can buy store-bought antipasti. They are already grilled and packed in their own oils, which adds lots more flavor. A selection of grilled vegetables could include artichokes, peppers, eggplant, pumpkin and sun-dried tomatoes. You can also add my Pepe Arrostiti (page 22) over the top.

To cover the base of this pizza I've used 5 tablespoons (75 ml) of my homemade basil oil—which you can find in the recipe on page 119—but if you want to change it up, basil or kale pesto would work just as well. The herb sauce will bring out the flavor of the vegetables and provide a gorgeous green hue. Try my homemade Hazelnut Pesto Sauce on page 20.

Fresh mozzarella is always a hit on homemade pizza. If you want an extra-creamy pizza, then burrata is the way to go. I find that prepackaged cheese tends to burn quite quickly during the baking process, which is why I always recommend using fresh.

Ingredients

1 batch Homemade Pizza Dough (page 38)

3 tbsp (45 ml) extra virgin olive oil, divided

1 medium eggplant, stem removed and thinly sliced lengthwise

1 medium zucchini, thinly sliced lengthwise

Salt and freshly ground black pepper

6 tbsp (90 ml) Homemade Basil Oil (page 119), divided

¼ red onion, thinly sliced

2.5 oz (70 g) fresh buffalo mozzarella, torn

1 oz (30 g) fresh arugula leaves

A handful of fresh basil leaves

Method

Make the Homemade Pizza Dough.

Lightly coat a 12 x 18–inch (30 x 45–cm) baking sheet with 2 tablespoons (30 ml) of olive oil and stretch out the dough to cover the base of the sheet.

Preheat the oven to 400°F (200°C). Toss the sliced eggplant and zucchini with the remaining olive oil and season well with salt and pepper. Heat a grill pan over medium-to-high heat and work in batches to grill the eggplant and zucchini until slightly charred, about 4 to 5 minutes on both sides. If adding vegetables such as pumpkin or sweet potatoes, slice them thinly, then coat them with a little olive oil, season them with salt and pepper and roast them in the oven for 25 to 30 minutes, until soft. They will continue to cook and caramelize once they are placed on top of the pizza base.

To assemble, drizzle 3 tablespoons (45 ml) of the Homemade Basil Oil or your choice of herb sauce all over the base of the pizza. Arrange the grilled eggplant and zucchini evenly, followed by the sliced red onion. If you're using store-bought antipasti, drain a little of the olive oil and add it to the top of the pizza. Over the years, I've actually added the marinated olive oil the antipasti are packaged in. It's a great way to use up all the ingredients, and it tastes amazing!

Put the pizza in the oven and bake for 20 to 25 minutes. Remove the pizza from the oven and add the torn mozzarella over the top. Put the pizza back into the oven and bake for 10 more minutes, or until the cheese has melted.

To serve, add the fresh arugula and basil leaves and drizzle the remaining basil oil over the top.

Prosciutto Crudo e Rucola

The fresh and light *prosciutto crudo e rucola* ("raw prosciutto and arugula") is one of my favorites. The sweet and delicate prosciutto used here is *crudo* (raw) and is added to the pizza after it's done baking, right before you slice the pizza.

When you purchase your prosciutto, you want to make sure that it's thinly sliced. If you cannot find prosciutto, a good alternative is smoked ham, as it tastes similar and works well with most ingredients.

Fresh arugula is used on top of this pizza, but a leafy green such as 1 cup (30 g) of baby spinach will work wonderfully. Watercress, which has a pungent peppery flavor, is also a good substitute. Radicchio leaves offer a nice change of pace in the taste department. They are sharp and bitter and are best when eaten raw. Use 2 cups (60 g) or less of either watercress or radicchio.

Adding thinly shaved Parmesan cheese is also key, as it offers a tangy, nutty flavor that works really well with the prosciutto and arugula. You can also use either pecorino or grana padano. My Mum's Homemade Sugo di Pomodoro (page 14) or 1 (14-ounce [400-g]) can of diced tomatoes can be used for the base.

If you add the prosciutto on top of the pizza prior to cooking, keep in mind it will not really be classified as a pizza crudo but will instead resemble a pizza *cotto*, which means "cooked." Either way you choose to serve this pizza, I guarantee you'll make it time and time again.

→ **Makes 1 large pizza** ←

Ingredients

1 batch Homemade Pizza Dough (page 38)

2 tbsp (30 ml) extra virgin olive oil, plus more for drizzling

1½ cups (360 ml) Mum's Homemade Sugo di Pomodoro (page 14)

4 oz (125 g) fresh mozzarella, drained and torn

8 slices prosciutto or smoked ham

2 cups (40 g) loosely packed arugula or baby spinach

Shaved Parmigiano cheese, for garnish

Freshly ground black pepper

Method

Make the Homemade Pizza Dough.

Lightly coat a 12 x 18–inch (30 x 45–cm) baking sheet with the olive oil and stretch out the dough to cover the base of the sheet.

Preheat the oven to 400°F (200°C). Spoon the sauce evenly over the base of the pizza, making sure it is completely covered. Alternatively, use your choice of tomato base, such as diced tomatoes or fresh cherry tomatoes cooked down. See my Classic Margherita Pizza recipe (page 72) for a simple method for making a delicious sauce.

Put the pizza in the oven and bake for 20 to 25 minutes. Remove the pizza from the oven and add the torn mozzarella over the top. Put the pizza back into the oven and bake for 10 more minutes, or until the cheese has melted.

Remove the pizza from the oven and add the fresh slices of prosciutto or ham evenly over the top. Add the arugula along with a generous amount of Parmesan shavings as a garnish.

Drizzle a generous amount of olive oil and freshly ground black pepper before slicing and serving.

Swiss Chard & Mushroom Calzones

A delicious on-the-go type of pizza, calzones are sold all over the streets of Italy. Many Italians love this delicious cheesy pocket due to the fact that they can eat it while walking without any fuss. More commonly, they are baked in the oven like a traditional pizza, although they are also known to be deep fried in hot oil, which creates a crunchy case filled with a melting cheesy center.

Traditionally, calzones are made with bread dough that is baked in the oven like a pizza. They are filled with glorious ingredients, including smoked ham, mozzarella, spinach, hot salami and so many other wonderful ingredients. When it comes to the quantities that go into a calzone filling, it can be quite subjective, as many Italian cooks like to use their instincts. Be careful not to overfill these, as they can rupture while baking.

You could use any of the recipes listed in this chapter to create mini calzones. There is absolutely no rule saying you should stick with a cheese-and-sauce combo. Choose from my list or other popular suggestions: goat cheese, grilled salmon and baby spinach leaves; or crispy bacon, boiled eggs and some of your favorite veggies.

Calzones don't fall solely into the savory category. Create a sweet alternative by including Nutella, sliced banana and walnuts. Spread 2 tablespoons (37 g) or more of Nutella over the base and cover with a few slices of banana and a sprinkle of crushed walnuts. An even more decadent option would be to add fresh raspberries and white chocolate with a final dusting of confectioners' sugar. It is a wonderful way to get the kids involved in the kitchen.

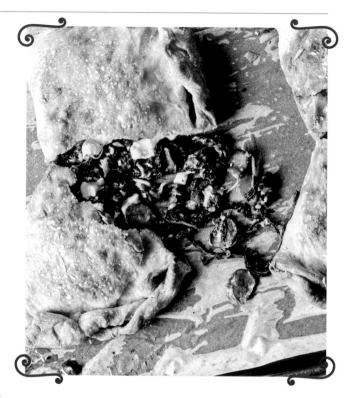

Ingredients

1 batch Homemade Pizza Dough (page 38)

3 tbsp (45 ml) extra virgin olive oil, plus more for brushing

12 oz (340 g) white mushrooms, sliced

2 cloves garlic, finely sliced

1 small white onion, finely diced

1 bunch Swiss chard, rinsed, stems removed and chopped into ½-inch (1.3-cm) pieces

1 tsp dried red pepper flakes

1 tsp dried oregano

Salt and freshly ground black pepper

1¼ cups (140 g) grated fontina cheese

½ cup (125 g) ricotta cheese

½ cup (50 g) grated Parmesan cheese

Method

Make the Homemade Pizza Dough, and divide the dough into eight equal pieces. If you prefer, you can make four bigger calzones instead of mini ones. Shape the dough into little balls so they are easier to roll into an even, round shape. Roll out your dough to about ¼ inch (6 mm) thick, keeping all 8 relatively the same in size.

Preheat the oven to 400°F (200°C). Line two 12 x 18–inch (30 x 45–cm) baking sheets with parchment paper.

Heat a saucepan over medium heat. Add the olive oil and cook the mushrooms in batches. Mushrooms hold a lot of liquid, so to achieve a golden color, give them enough room in the saucepan and enough time to brown and caramelize. Once all the mushrooms have browned, transfer them to a small bowl.

In the same saucepan, over low heat, add a little more oil if needed and then add the garlic and onion. Sauté for 2 to 3 minutes, stirring occasionally, until the onion is soft and translucent. Add the Swiss chard or your choice of leafy greens and stir until the greens have wilted. Add the cooked mushrooms back in along with the red pepper flakes, oregano, salt and pepper, and stir to combine.

Remove from the heat and allow to cool in the saucepan. Once cooled, stir in the grated fontina and set aside.

To assemble the calzones: Spread 1 tablespoon (16 g) of ricotta evenly in the center of each of the dough bases. Spoon 2 tablespoons (32 g) of the Swiss chard–mushroom mixture evenly on one side of the dough, making sure you leave ½ inch (1.3 cm) around the edges. Evenly sprinkle grated Parmesan over the filling. Carefully fold in half, then press down on the edges to seal them.

If you are working with alternative fillings, whether savory or sweet, evenly divide these onto each of the bases, making sure you have an equal amount and that you have enough room around the edges. Make sure each one is sealed well to prevent the filling from escaping while it bakes. Fold the edges in, like you would for a dumpling, or you can use a fork to crimp the edges.

Transfer to the prepared baking sheets. Brush each of the calzones with a little olive oil and put the baking sheets into the oven for 20 to 25 minutes, or until the tops have puffed up and are golden brown. Serve the calzones immediately.

Chapter Four

From the Land to the Sea

The meat and fish dishes featured in the following chapter make up the essence of Italian cooking. These meals are prepared with care, slow cooked or roasted in their own juices, and create enticing aromas in the kitchen.

In this chapter there are more meat dishes than fish, which I think stems from my southern Italian heritage. My family uses lots of beef and pork in their cooking, so it was only natural that I found more comfort in cooking more of these types of dishes. I love making these, as they focus on the simplicity of Italian cooking: creating bold flavors and using what herbs and spices the modern-day cook has already in their kitchen.

Beef Braciole (page 102) is a family favorite, and we sometimes add it to a simmering pasta sauce. The filling is kept quite simple, but there are lots of alternatives that can be incorporated. Slow-Roasted Lamb Shoulder (page 88) is made on very special occasions. It's covered in fresh rosemary and garlic, although it can include other earthy ingredients to suit your palate. You will love the Pane e Porchetta (page 100), with its signature crackling, peppery taste and a burst of citrus.

I really do urge you to try your own different flavors in the kitchen, as this is the best way to discover what you and your family really enjoy. Who knows, you may even conjure an iconic dish that your family will talk about for years to come.

Slow-Roasted Lamb Shoulder

This juicy and succulent slow-roasted lamb shoulder will melt in your mouth. A wonderful combination of herbs, citrus and garlic brings this cut of meat to life. Italian slow-roasted lamb contains very simple ingredients, but use your intuition and experiment with different taste combinations to create your own slow roast.

If you want to take a more Middle Eastern approach, ground cumin provides an earthy tang. I suggest using 1 teaspoon for a 3½-pound (1.5-kg) piece of lamb, as you don't want to overpower the meat with the spice.

Avoid using garlic powder to replace fresh garlic. Garlic powder has a very distinct and intense flavor that can be quite strong and potentially ruin the dish. For a sweeter addition, try a tablespoon (15 ml) of honey or (15 g) of brown sugar or use an orange, which will really bring out the flavor of the lamb. Some dry red wine will deepen the flavors even more. The combination of the fat from the lamb with the olive oil and wine will create a syrupy sauce.

Slow-roasted lamb needs to be cooked at a consistent temperature. A higher temperature will quickly toughen up the meat, so the key is to keep it consistent throughout the cooking process. I love to prepare the lamb shoulder 24 hours prior to cooking, as it helps all the flavors to intensify overnight, and I can just pop it into the oven the next day. Feel free to substitute the lamb shoulder with pork or beef shoulder. Pork works really well with fennel seeds, peppercorns and lemon zest. When roasting beef, use rosemary, sage and thyme.

Ingredients

3½ lb (1.5 kg) lamb shoulder, bone in

2 cloves garlic, thinly sliced

1 bulb garlic, cloves separated and skins on

1 sprig rosemary, stalk removed and leaves roughly chopped

Zest and juice of 1 lemon

Salt and freshly ground black pepper

Generous amount of extra virgin olive oil

2 tbsp (15 g) cornstarch

Method

Allow the meat to come to room temperature. Leave out for about 1 hour prior to roasting, as this will help the meat to cook evenly.

Preheat the oven to 350°F (175°C). Prepare the lamb by patting it down with a paper towel to remove any excess moisture. Leave the fat on the lamb, as this will render during the cooking process and make it extra tasty. However, you can trim down as much of the fat as you like.

Put the lamb in the center of a large baking dish and use a knife to score the top of the lamb. Insert the garlic slices into each of the incisions and scatter the cloves from the bulb all around and underneath the meat. Cooking the garlic cloves in their skins protects them from burning and caramelizes them, creating a perfect complement to the meat.

Scatter the rosemary or your choice of fresh or dried herbs, such as thyme or oregano, all over and underneath the lamb, including the little incisions. Grate the lemon zest all over the lamb, then squeeze the juice over the meat. For a sweeter option, replace the lemon zest and juice with those of an orange or a drizzle of honey. Add the spent citrus halves into the baking dish along with the lamb, if desired.

Season well with salt and pepper, and drizzle a generous amount of good-quality olive oil all over the meat. If you're going with Middle Eastern flavors, I suggest mixing spices such as cumin with the olive oil. This will coat the lamb with the spices more evenly.

Work the oil and herbs into the meat with your hands, making sure the entire piece of lamb is completely covered. As previously mentioned, this step can be done the night before to intensify the flavors. If you'd like to add a little red wine, pour about a ½ cup (120 ml) into the bottom of the baking tray just before popping it into the oven.

Put it in the oven to roast for up to 4 hours, basting every hour with the juices. The lamb is ready when the meat is tender and falling off the bone. Remove it from the oven and allow to rest for 30 minutes before serving.

Remove the lamb shoulder from the baking dish and allow it to rest on a clean surface. Remove the citrus halves and transfer the whole garlic cloves to a bowl. Put the baking dish with all the juices back into the oven for 10 minutes with a few tablespoons (about 15 g) of cornstarch for a thicker consistency. Once whisked and thickened, pour the sauce into a gravy boat for serving.

Arrange the lamb on a serving dish accompanied by the caramelized garlic and the sauce.

Nonna Rosa's Osso Buco

Osso buco is the ultimate winter comfort food. Cooked low and slow for a rich and deep flavor, this dish is very popular throughout Italy. This recipe is one of my nonna's specialties, and it is most definitely a family favorite. Every time she makes this dish, she gets it spot-on. We serve our osso buco over creamy mashed potatoes or polenta with a generous serving of the pan juices spooned over the top.

Osso buco originates from the Lombardy region in northern Italy. It's made from a crosscut veal shank and braised with hearty vegetables and seasoned stock. It is sometimes served with fresh gremolata (page 107) and Risotto alla Milanese (page 142). It is very well known for the marrow in the center bone, which can be eaten on its own or added to mashed potatoes.

I like to put the veal shanks into two 13 x 9–inch (33 x 23–cm) rectangular baking dishes, as it helps the meat to cook evenly. Baking in the oven for a minimum of 2 hours allows the veal to become super tender and fall-off-the-bone. If veal shanks are not readily available, or you prefer another type of meat, beef shanks will work just as well. Alternatively, you can use short ribs or gravy beef cut into large pieces. Try to use beef stock in this recipe, as it really brings out the flavor. If you have chicken stock you can use it, but it will change the taste of the dish completely. Vegetable stock, however, has a more natural flavor that won't overpower the taste; use 2 cups (480 ml).

If you have some plum tomatoes lying around, dice them and use them in addition to the canned tomatoes. Carrots and celery are a must when cooking osso buco, and you can feel free to add 1 or 2 diced potatoes or sweet potatoes. I recommend using the celery leaves, as they are quite nutritious and packed with flavor.

Browning the meat is one of the most important parts of this recipe. Releasing the veal's natural juices adds so much flavor to the dish. The sauce is spooned over the veal just before serving, but you could also reduce even further by simmering it for 10 minutes over low heat in a saucepan. Add a couple of tablespoons (15 g) of flour or corn flour, as this will thicken it and create a delicious gravy.

You can also make gremolata to serve with the lamb—a colorful and tasty addition.

Ingredients

6 veal shanks, crosscut into 1½-inch (4-cm) pieces

Salt and freshly ground black pepper

½ cup (60 g) all-purpose flour

5 tbsp (75 ml) extra virgin olive oil, plus more for searing

1 large carrot, peeled and chopped

1 large rib celery, leaves included, chopped

½ medium red or green bell pepper, chopped

1 white onion, cut into quarters

3 large cloves garlic, peeled and kept whole

1 tbsp (15 g) unsalted butter

1 (14-oz [400-g]) can diced tomatoes

1 cup (240 ml) red wine

1 cup (240 ml) dry white wine

2 cups (480 ml) beef stock, plus more if needed

2 bay leaves

1 tbsp (2 g) fresh rosemary leaves

Method

Preheat the oven to 356°F (180°C).

Place the veal shanks into two 13 x 9–inch (33 x 23–cm) rectangular baking dishes. Season the meat (short ribs or gravy beef cuts if you're not using veal) with a generous amount of salt and pepper.

Add the flour into a shallow bowl and dip the shanks one by one into the flour, coating them lightly on both sides. Dust off any excess flour and set the shanks aside. In a large saucepan, heat some olive oil over medium-to-high heat. Working in batches, sear each side of veal until nicely browned all over, about 2 to 3 minutes per side. Remove from the heat and evenly distribute the shanks into the two baking dishes.

In the same saucepan, over medium-low heat, add the carrot, celery, bell pepper, onion, garlic and butter. If you'd like, add potatoes or sweet potatoes with the other vegetables. As the vegetables cook and soften, scrape up the caramelized bits left over from browning the meat from the bottom of the saucepan, as it has so much flavor. Cook the vegetables for about 2 to 3 minutes, until they are slightly soft. Remove the pan from the heat.

(continued)

Nonna Rosa's Osso Buco (Continued)

Spread the vegetables evenly over the shanks, including any pan juices. This is where all the flavor is! Evenly pour the tomatoes, red wine, white wine and stock between the two dishes. Season well with the bay leaves, rosemary, salt and pepper. Alternatively, add different herbs and spices, such as fresh or dried oregano or some dried red pepper flakes for some heat.

Cover with a layer of parchment paper, followed by aluminum foil wrapped tightly. Covering the veal while it bakes is important, as it helps keep it succulent and super tasty. I recommend doing the same for larger cuts of meats including lamb, beef or pork. For smaller cuts such as short ribs, I suggest leaving them uncovered in the oven, keeping an eye on the liquid throughout the cooking process.

Bake at 356°F (180°C) for 30 minutes, then reduce the heat to 325°F (160°C) for 1½ hours, checking the liquid occasionally. If you feel the stock has cooked down quickly, add a little more. I love to spoon the liquid over each of the shanks during the cooking process, as it helps keep the meat moist and tender. Repeat this two or three times during the cooking process. If you like, you can remove the foil and parchment paper for the last 30 minutes of cooking to reduce the liquid further for a much thicker sauce. Pierce a shank with a fork to test for tenderness; it will fall apart when ready.

I like to serve my osso buco on a large platter or kept in the baking dish surrounded by the thick sauce. Serve over creamy mashed potatoes or polenta and top with a few tablespoons of fresh homemade gremolata (page 107), if desired.

Italian Meatballs Three Ways

Meatballs are adored worldwide, and I absolutely love making and of course eating them. There are many different takes in various cultures, and they can be filled with literally anything that you can imagine. We have all come to know the famous dish of spaghetti and meatballs, but it is actually not traditional in Italian cuisine. They are more commonly cooked in the sauce while it's simmering. This helps to intensify the flavor of the sauce, which is another little trick us Italians like to do. Meatballs, called polpette, are traditionally fried and served on their own, or they can be added to soups. These delicious polpette are found quite commonly all over Italy and are not specific to any region, but they have been adapted to highlight popular regional ingredients. In the northern regions, people are known to add leftover roasted veal or beef to their polpette, and down in the south, ground chuck steak or sometimes sausage is used. The sky's the limit when making polpette, and you may add any meat you like.

When I was growing up, my family made traditional meatballs for Saturday dinner that were filled with ground beef, Parmesan, garlic and parsley. The intense smell coming from my nonna's kitchen would travel outside to the street. I would find myself salivating at the front door before I had even entered the house. For a really quick and easy meal for the week, I always turn to making them. It might be just me, but I find it so therapeutic to make meatballs.

Meatballs make a super-versatile dish, and you can add a variety of ingredients you have in your kitchen. Of course, staple ingredients of bread crumbs, egg, grated cheese, garlic and oil are required, but you can add just about any other ingredient you want. You can cook polpette a few different ways as well. I love to fry mine in a little olive oil, as I love the outer crunch that develops after the meat hits the hot oil. You can also bake then in the oven for a healthier alternative, or add them to a simmering sauce such as my Mum's Homemade Sugo di Pomodoro (page 14) for the last 30 minutes of cooking.

The elements that make up meatballs are very simple and can be altered to include what you have on hand. Start with a fairly solid protein such as ground beef or chicken or, for a vegetarian twist, vegetables such as zucchini and eggplant, which makes up the bulk of the mixture. You want an ingredient that is sturdy and hearty so it holds together when you're molding the meatballs. If you are using ingredients that hold lots of water, such as eggplant or zucchini, make sure you remove as much moisture as you can.

I use a combination of dried bread crumbs and bread soaked in milk in my polpette. The milk-soaked bread acts as a binding agent and adds flavor as well as a soft and tender texture. Dried bread crumbs also act as a binding agent and help balance out the wetness of the soaked bread, making it much easier to shape your polpette. If you prefer not to use the milk-soaked bread, you can add ½ cup (54 g) of dried bread crumbs to the mixture.

There are no rules when it comes to making meatballs, so you can be as creative as you like. I've included three simple ways of cooking polpette over the next pages.

Beef Meatballs

This classic Italian meatball recipe is one I've been following for years. It's a simple yet very quick and easy base to begin with and it takes almost no time at all to prepare and cook. Freeze them individually in airtight containers to be used at a later date or for when you need to put together a really fast dinner.

These meatballs are made with ground beef, but adding two different types of meat can be a really great option. Try ½ pound (226 g) of ground beef and ½ pound (226 g) of ground veal. Lots of Italian cooks mix these two together, as veal is more tender than beef and creates a lovely texture and also adds a lot of flavor. To incorporate some vegetables into the mixture, finely dice 1 or 2 small carrots or finely chop 2 or 3 big handfuls of baby spinach. Using frozen spinach is absolutely fine, but squeeze out as much liquid as possible, as spinach contains lots of water.

These beef meatballs need some form of grated cheese to help bind the mixture together. I love using a mix of grated Parmesan and pecorino as the two combined have a robust nutty, salty flavor. Alternatively, grated grana padano is a good choice. If you want these meatballs to be extra cheesy, some shredded mozzarella is your best option.

Ingredients

4 slices (100 g) day-old bread, roughly torn

⅓ cup (80 ml) whole milk

1 lb (454 g) lean ground beef

1 cup (108 g) dried bread crumbs

1 tbsp (3 g) dried oregano

½ cup (50 g) grated Parmesan cheese

½ cup (50 g) grated pecorino cheese

1 egg, beaten

2 cloves garlic, minced

¼ cup (15 g) fresh parsley, chopped

Salt and freshly ground black pepper

Olive oil, for frying or baking

Method

Put the torn bread into a bowl and pour the milk over it, making sure it is completely covered. Soak the bread for 5 to 10 minutes, until it is soft but not falling apart. Remove any excess milk from the bread by gently squeezing out the liquid with your hands.

Transfer the soaked bread to a large, clean bowl and add the ground beef, dried bread crumbs, oregano, Parmesan, pecorino, egg, garlic and parsley. Add any extra ingredients to the mixture, if using, such as shredded mozzarella, bocconcini, carrots or spinach. Season with salt and pepper and mix well with your hands, making sure everything is combined. Add any extra herbs or spices of your choice at this time. Keep it fairly simple and stick with the same amount suggested for the oregano. Try cumin and smoked paprika for more spice. If the mixture seems too wet, add a small amount of bread crumbs or grated Parmesan or pecorino.

Line a 12 x 18–inch (30 x 45–cm) baking sheet with parchment paper. I use my hands to measure out a rough size of each of my meatballs, but you can use a tablespoon if you prefer. With your hands, gently roll the meatballs into golf ball–sized shapes. Shaping meatballs is subjective, and you can make them as small or large as you want. Whichever size you prefer, keep them all relatively the same size to ensure that they cook evenly.

Lay the meatballs onto the parchment-lined baking sheet, cover with plastic wrap, and refrigerate for an hour. This helps them retain their shape during the cooking process. As mentioned previously, freezing these separately and placing them into airtight containers is a great way to meal prep for the future. Allow the meatballs to thaw completely before cooking or adding them to anything else.

To panfry the meatballs, heat a little olive oil in a large saucepan over low-to-medium heat. Fry the meatballs for 10 to 12 minutes, turning often to cook each of the sides evenly, until golden brown and cooked through.

To cook them in sauce, prepare my Mum's Homemade Sugo di Pomodoro (page 14) and add the meatballs for the last 30 minutes of cooking time.

To bake them, preheat the oven to 350°F (175°C). Brush or drizzle the meatballs with a little olive oil, put them on a parchment-lined baking sheet and bake for 20 to 25 minutes, until golden brown.

I love to serve the meatballs with my Panzanella (page 132) or Buttery Parmesan-Roasted Potatoes (page 140).

Pork & Fennel Meatballs

Pork and fennel are a perfect combination. The fragrance of the seeds brings a warm, sweet aroma. The anise flavor not only tastes incredible but also enhances the salty pork. It is no wonder that these two standout ingredients are so commonly used in Italian cooking.

I typically use a lean ground pork, but feel free to use any type of ground meat you prefer, perhaps trying beef or chicken for a different flavor. Of course, be more mindful of the cooking method when using lean ground meat, as the meatballs can dry out when you fry or bake them. That is why I usually add these meatballs to other recipes that help them retain their shape and moisture, such as simmering sauces or soups. Ground veal is an excellent substitute for pork because it is more similar in taste than ground chicken or turkey. You could even combine pork and veal, using ½ pound (226 g) of each for a different combination of flavors.

Fennel seeds are really the partnering hero when it comes to pork, but another spice that has a similar taste to fennel is cumin seed, which is also a great option. You can use the same amount of cumin as you would fennel. As you've probably noticed by now, I love adding heat to my dishes, so I will sometimes add 1 teaspoon or more of dried red pepper flakes or a fresh chile that has been deseeded and finely chopped.

Sage leaves also pair really well with pork. Adding a generous handful of roughly chopped sage leaves will not only taste delicious but also give your meatballs a rustic feel. For a citrus twist, adding some freshly grated lemon zest works well with the combination of the pork and fennel and provides a touch of brightness.

Makes 15 to 20 meatballs

Ingredients

1 tbsp (6 g) fennel seeds

4 slices (100 g) day-old bread, roughly torn

⅓ cup (80 ml) whole milk

1 lb (454 g) ground pork

1 tsp dried red pepper flakes

¼ cup (15 g) finely chopped parsley

½ cup (50 g) grated Parmesan cheese

½ cup (50 g) grated pecorino cheese

½ cup (50 g) dried bread crumbs

1 egg, beaten

Salt and freshly ground black pepper

Method

In this recipe I have added the fennel seeds without toasting them. The heat from toasting the fennel seeds, or others such as cumin seeds will release their natural oils. If you would like to toast them, add the fennel to a large saucepan over medium heat and cook for 1 to 2 minutes, until slightly golden and fragrant. Allow to cool completely before adding them to the remaining ingredients.

Line a 12 x 18–inch (30 x 45–cm) baking sheet with parchment paper. Put the torn bread into a bowl and pour the milk over it, making sure it is completely covered. Soak the bread for 5 to 10 minutes, until it is soft but not falling apart. Remove excess milk from the bread by gently squeezing out the liquid with your hands.

Transfer the soaked bread to a large, clean bowl and add the ground pork, fennel seeds, red pepper flakes, parsley, Parmesan, pecorino, bread crumbs and egg, and season with salt and pepper. Add or replace any of the herbs and spices with others such as as cumin, fresh herbs or lemon zest. Use your hands to mix well, making sure everything is combined. If the mixture seems too wet, add a small amount of bread crumbs or grated cheese.

Use your hands to shape the meatballs, making sure that they are all relatively the same size. Put the meatballs onto the parchment-lined baking sheet, cover them with plastic wrap and refrigerate for up to one hour. This helps them retain their shape, so they will not fall apart during the cooking process. As mentioned, freezing these separately and placing them into airtight containers is a great way to meal prep for the future.

I love to add these pork and fennel meatballs to simmering soups and sauces and serve them in baked dishes, such as Ziti al Forno (page 54), or you could even use them in my Orecchiette with Broccoli & Sausages (page 58) as a replacement for the sausages.

To panfry the meatballs, heat a little olive oil in a large saucepan over low-to-medium heat. Fry the meatballs for 10 to 12 minutes, turning often to cook each of the sides evenly, until golden brown and cooked through.

To bake them, preheat the oven to 350°F (175°C). Brush or drizzle the meatballs with a little olive oil, put them on the parchment-lined baking sheet and bake for 20 to 25 minutes, until golden brown.

Eggplant Balls

Eggplant is such a flexible ingredient, and it can be cooked many different ways. Traditionally, it is used to make eggplant Parmesan *(parmigiana di melanzane)*, which is delicious in its own right. My nonna makes stuffed eggplant, which are hollow and filled with ground beef, Parmesan cheese, rice and bread crumbs and baked until golden brown. You cannot stop at just one. Another way to use eggplant is in *polpettine di melanzana,* or eggplant balls. It is a traditional cucina povera southern Italian dish that is made just like meatballs, with cheese, bread crumbs and egg.

These are best enjoyed fried. It must be the combination of the golden crispy eggplant and the cheeses that make them so tasty. I fry them in olive oil, which gives them their crispy outer edge. I also use a classic method of salting the diced eggplant and letting them rest for 10 minutes, which helps to remove some of the water before you pat them down with a paper towel. Eggplant has tough flesh, so cooking it down in a little olive oil also helps to soften it, which makes it easier to mix in with the remaining ingredients. I personally like to use the eggplant skin as well, but if you prefer, you can peel this off prior to dicing.

I keep the seasoning fairly simple, but you can add what you like to enhance the flavor of the dish even more. A generous handful of fresh basil leaves complements eggplant well; roughly chop 3 tablespoons (5 g) or add 1 tablespoon (5 g) of dried basil into the mixture. I love to add fresh parsley, as it always brings so much flavor. Because eggplant has a high water content, I would steer clear of using soft cheeses such as mozzarella, as it can lead to the eggplant balls falling apart. Stick to hard cheeses such as Parmesan or pecorino to help keep the mixture together.

Ingredients

1 lb (454 g) eggplant, cut into 1½-inch (4-cm) cubes

Salt

2 tbsp (30 ml) extra virgin olive oil, plus more
for frying or drizzling

Freshly ground black pepper

4 slices (100 g) day-old bread, roughly torn

⅓ cup (80 ml) whole milk

1 egg, beaten

½ cup (50 g) grated Parmesan cheese

½ cup (50 g) grated pecorino cheese

1¼ cups (135 g) dried bread crumbs

1 tsp dried red pepper flakes

¼ cup (15 g) fresh parsley, chopped

2 cloves garlic, minced

Method

Sprinkle the cubed eggplant with a little salt. Allow the cubes to sit for 10 to 15 minutes to draw out any excess moisture. Pat them dry with a paper towel.

Heat a large saucepan over low-to-medium heat. Add the eggplant, olive oil, salt and pepper and cook until the eggplant becomes soft and tender, about 15 to 20 minutes. Use a fork to gently press on them; this helps them cook down. Remove from the heat and allow to cool completely.

Meanwhile, line a 12 x 18–inch (30 x 45–cm) baking sheet with parchment paper. Add the torn bread to a bowl and pour the milk over it, making sure it's completely covered. Soak for 5 to 10 minutes, until the bread is soft but not falling apart. Squeeze out any excess milk from the bread, and add the soaked bread to the cooled eggplant. Add the egg, Parmesan, pecorino, bread crumbs, red pepper flakes, parsley, garlic and additional salt and pepper, and use your hands to combine everything. If the mixture is slightly wet, add a few tablespoons (15 g) of dried bread crumbs or grated cheese to the mixture. If the mixture is dry, a little water will loosen it up.

Spoon out 2-tablespoon-sized (30-ml) amounts of the mixture, and, using your hands, gently roll into golf ball–sized shapes. You can make them any size you like, just make sure that they are all relatively the same size to ensure they cook evenly. Put them on the parchment-lined baking sheet, cover with plastic wrap and refrigerate for up to an hour.

I like to fry these eggplant balls in a little olive oil using a large saucepan over low-to-medium heat. Fry them for 10 to 12 minutes, turning them often to cook each side evenly, until they are golden and crispy. You can place them on a platter and serve them as an antipasto with my Fresh & Simple Bruschetta (page 116) or alongside my Roasted Mediterranean Vegetables (page 134).

To bake, preheat the oven to 350°F (175°C). Brush or drizzle the meatballs with a little olive oil, put them on the parchment-lined baking sheet and bake for 20 to 25 minutes, until golden brown.

Have these for a meatless dinner with some homemade pasta sauce. Fry them for about 10 minutes to get the outside nice and brown before adding them to the simmering sauce.

Pane e Porchetta

If you walk along the cobbled streets of Italy, you will find the most delicious takeaway sandwich known to man. I am talking about none other than pane e porchetta. Pane e porchetta is a rich, full-flavored meal found at Italian festivals and street stalls. Originating from the central regions of Italy, it dates back to Roman times and is popular to this day.

The hero of the dish is, of course, the *porchetta* (the pork shoulder). It's a relatively inexpensive cut that is available with or without the bone. I like to use boneless pork shoulder, as it's so much easier to slice, but bone-in can add so much more flavor. I've kept the spice rub relatively simple, but you can most definitely add to it or make up your own. I like to add all my spice ingredients into a mortar and pestle and grind them down to achieve a fine grain. You can toast the seeds prior to grinding to add even more depth of flavor.

Experiment with different dried herbs, such as 1 teaspoon each of dried thyme and oregano. They both contain a peppery, yet minty flavor that is a perfect combination with pork. Another great herb is fresh sage, and fennel would complement this nicely. Roughly chop a generous handful of both and add them to the filling.

Pork crackling! There is nothing like it, and it wouldn't be porchetta without it. To achieve this, you need to prep the pork prior to roasting. This means the fat cap on the pork shoulder needs to be dried out extremely well. Pat down with a paper towel to remove any excess moisture from the fat and keep it uncovered in the fridge. This will allow the fat to dry out completely, and once it's popped into the oven, it will react to the heat and achieve the crispy skin that you want.

The pork is slow roasted for 3½ to 4 hours, but the first 25 to 30 minutes of cooking is when you want to get a start on that crispy skin, so start with an extremely hot oven. I love to add this slow-cooked porchetta to crusty ciabatta rolls, but you can serve this porchetta alongside my Roasted Mediterranean Vegetables (page 134) or Buttery Parmesan-Roasted Potatoes (page 140).

Ingredients

2 tsp (4 g) fennel seeds

Zest of 1 lemon

1 tsp dried rosemary

½ tsp black peppercorns

2 cloves garlic, minced

½ tsp dried red pepper flakes

1 tbsp (30 g) sea salt

¼ cup (60 ml) extra virgin olive oil

3½ lb (1.5 kg) boneless pork shoulder with fat cap

Crusty ciabatta rolls

Method

I like to prepare the pork shoulder a day in advance. This is to make sure the skin is dried out completely in order to achieve that crispy crackling skin.

First, you want to make the spiced rub by adding the fennel seeds, lemon zest, rosemary, peppercorns, garlic, red pepper flakes and sea salt into a mortar and pestle. Pound vigorously until it forms a paste-like texture. If you don't have a mortar and pestle, put all the herbs into a ziplock bag, and use a rolling pin or the bottom of a drinking glass to gently press down on the herbs. Pour the olive oil in with the spice mix, stir and set aside.

Lay the pork flat on a clean surface with the fat-cap side facing up. Use a sharp knife to score the fat in a diamond-shaped pattern. Flip the pork over, with the fat-cap side facing down, and use your hands to work the spice rub into the meat, covering it entirely. Pork shoulder comes in many different shapes. Boston butt is a similar cut—it's actually part of the pork shoulder but higher up, and it is often sold in a more rectangular, thicker cut.

Put the pork, fat-cap side facing up, into a 13 x 9–inch (33 x 23–cm) baking dish and use a paper towel to remove any excess moisture from the fat side. Keep any liquid ingredients such as olive oil away from the fat cap once it's completely dried, as the liquid causes it to turn rubbery when it comes into contact with the heat. Keep it uncovered in the refrigerator for 24 hours prior to roasting.

Remove the pork from the refrigerator 1 hour prior to cooking to allow it to come to room temperature. Preheat the oven to 425°F (220°C), and put the pork into the oven to cook for 30 minutes. This will allow that crispy skin to develop. Reduce heat to 320°F (160°C) for the remaining 3 to 3½ hours. The pork will be soft, tender and will pull apart easily, and the fat cap will be crispy and golden brown.

Transfer the porchetta to a cutting board to rest for 30 minutes. Set aside the pan juices. Slice the meat into ¼-inch (6-mm) slices and return them to the baking dish with the juices. Grab yourself some crusty rolls and place a generous serving of porchetta into them. Don't forget to add a drizzle of those delicious juices from the baking dish.

Beef Braciole

Beef braciole is a hearty, home-style dish found through-out Italy. The beef steak is delicately flattened and filled with salty prosciutto, Parmesan cheese and garlic, then rolled and cooked in a tomato sauce.

Every family has their own unique version with their favorite fillings. My family fills our beef braciole with cheese, garlic and lots and lots of fresh parsley. Once these little parcels are secured, we cook them with our homemade sauce. The sauce is then tossed with the pasta, reserving the beef braciole for an instant second course. The term *braciola* means "beef wrapped around a seasoned filling." This method can also be used on other kinds of meat, such as chicken or pork.

You will use the same method of flattening the meat regardless of what kind of meat you choose. If you decide on chicken or pork, be mindful to pound the meat delicately, as you don't want to ruin the shape of each of the fillets. You want the pieces of meat to be roughly the same thickness, about ¼ inch (6 mm). There are numerous fillings for this very popular dish, so feel free to be creative with the ingredients you already have in your fridge. Try smoked ham slices instead of a prosciutto, for example.

This recipe calls for grated Parmesan cheese, but another hard cheese, such as Swiss or provolone, would also work. Avoid using soft cheeses with a high moisture content, such as mozzarella or Brie, as they could ooze out and potentially ruin the dish.

To create a heartier filling, try some fresh baby spinach or Pepe Arrostiti (page 22). This recipe calls for beef stock, but if you opt for pork or chicken, chicken or vegetable stock will work just as well.

I absolutely love this dish, as it reminds me of weekend lunches when I was a child, and every time I make it, it takes me right back.

Ingredients

1 cup (100 g) grated Parmesan cheese

½ cup (55 g) dried bread crumbs

2 tbsp (8 g) flat-leaf parsley, finely chopped, plus more for serving

4 cloves garlic, minced

Salt and freshly ground black pepper

2 lb (1 kg) beef flank steak, cut into 12 (¼-inch [6-mm]-thick) slices

12 thin slices prosciutto

¼ cup (60 ml) extra virgin olive oil

2 cloves garlic, thinly sliced

1 small white onion, finely diced

1 tbsp (16 g) tomato paste

½ cup (120 ml) beef stock

1½ cups (360 ml) Mum's Homemade Sugo di Pomodoro (page 14)

Method

To make the filling: Add the Parmesan cheese, bread crumbs, parsley, minced garlic and salt and pepper into a bowl, and use either a spoon or your hands to combine well, then set aside.

Use a meat mallet to pound the beef into a ¼-inch (6-mm) thickness. If the pieces of beef are thick, feel free to slice them in half through the middle.

There is really no right or wrong length when it comes to making braciole, but I like to keep them fairly uniform in size so they cook evenly in the sauce. Use the length of your hand as a general guide when cutting the pieces of meat, about 6 to 7 inches (15 to 18 cm) long.

Take a slice of prosciutto and lay it over the slice of beef, then add a spoonful of the bread crumb–Parmesan mixture over the top of the prosciutto. I like to flatten the filling a little with my hands to prevent it from falling out. Gently grab one side of the beef and slowly start to roll it into a log using a few toothpicks to secure the meat. You can use cooking twine if you have that on hand, but I use my family's method with toothpicks. Repeat with the remaining slices of prosciutto and filling until all of it has been used.

In a large saucepan, heat the olive oil over low-to-medium heat. Working in batches, sear the beef pieces until they are slightly golden all over, about 1 to 2 minutes on each side. Transfer the braciole to a plate. Add the sliced garlic and onion to the saucepan and cook for 2 to 3 minutes until the onion is translucent. Add the tomato paste, and cook for another 1 to 2 minutes, until fragrant.

Pour in the stock to deglaze the pan, making sure you scrape the bottom of the saucepan well to incorporate all the flavor from the meat. Pour in the homemade sauce, season with salt and pepper and stir it well.

Add the beef back into the saucepan. Cover and simmer for 25 to 30 minutes over low heat. Stir occasionally to prevent the beef from sticking to the bottom and allow the sauce to coat each little parcel.

To serve, remove the toothpicks and present them on a large platter, pouring the remaining sauce over them. If desired, scatter more freshly chopped parsley over the top.

Easy Oven-Roasted Sausages & Potatoes

This oven roast is a simple but very tasty dish that the entire family will enjoy. My family makes this all the time with pork sausages and baby potatoes. Serve it as the main event along with a garden salad or fresh green beans.

Italian sausages are used in this recipe, as I find they add lots of flavor when roasted and paired with potatoes. They often include seasonings such as fennel seeds, garlic and red pepper flakes, which are a fantastic combination, but feel free to use different sausages that you prefer or have on hand. You could even try 1 pound (454 g) of sliced chorizo for a little change. Chorizo packs a bit of a punch and pairs nicely with potatoes. Use other hot spicy sausages to give this dish some extra kick!

If potatoes aren't handy, most other root vegetables will work well. Using sweet potatoes, carrots, turnips, celeriac, yams or even squash are perfect substitutes. Feel free to use a combination of these vegetables, making sure is it roughly the same weight as the potatoes, 14 ounces (400 g).

Sometimes, I like to add white onion, sliced into quarters and nestled among the sausage and potatoes. Mixed with the olive oil and garlic, the onions will turn sticky and caramelize while they roast in the oven. If the bottom of the pan seems dry, add a little liquid—¼ cup (60 ml) of beef or chicken stock—to the bottom of the baking dish. This will help keep the meat and potatoes tender and juicy while cooking.

To make this a one-pan dish with fresh veggies, add cherry tomatoes attached to their vines—about 1 cup (150 g). I like using them from time to time, as the tomatoes blister while baking, and when mixed with the garlic, herbs and olive oil, it's a melt-in-your-mouth proposition.

Ingredients

1 lb (454 g) Italian sausage links, cut in half widthwise

14 oz (400 g) baby potatoes, skin on and sliced in half

2 cloves garlic, finely sliced

1 large white onion, cut into quarters

¼ cup (60 ml) extra virgin olive oil

Sprig of rosemary, stems removed and leaves roughly chopped

Salt and freshly ground black pepper

Method

Preheat the oven to 350°F (175°C). In a 13 x 9–inch (33 x 23–cm) baking dish, add the sausages, potatoes, garlic and onion. Using a deep dish keeps all the juices in while cooking. I find that a shallow baking dish tends to cause the meat to dry out a little.

If using alternative vegetables such as sweet potatoes, carrots, turnips, celeriac, squash or yams, rinse well to remove any dirt, remove the ends and peel the skin, if desired. I keep the skin on my potatoes, as it gives them an extra-crispy element when baked in the oven, but you can peel them, if you prefer.

Add the olive oil, rosemary or your choice of spices. Season well with salt and pepper, and use your hands to give it a good mix. If you have added any extra vegetables to the dish and it is looking a little full, evenly divide them among two roasting pans, making sure everything is layered evenly so all the ingredients cook through.

Put the dish in the oven and cook for 1 hour. After 30 minutes, gently stir the sausages and potatoes, and continue cooking for another 30 minutes, or until the sausages are golden brown and the potatoes are tender when pierced with a fork. Serve on a large platter alongside steamed green beans with garlic, olive oil and fresh mint.

Baked Cod with Cherry Tomatoes & Gremolata

Keep it super simple with delicious baked cod surrounded by blistered cherry tomatoes and homemade gremolata. This dish is the perfect way to eat your way through Sunday lunch, accompanied with a glass or two of white wine.

Gremolata is a classic Italian condiment that's extremely versatile, since you can pair it with almost any meat or seafood dish. It's made up of fresh parsley, garlic, lemon and olive oil. You can add ½ cup (around 70 g) of pine nuts, hazelnuts or almonds for some crunch. The lemon adds a zesty tang along with a wonderful burst of color. A good gremolata thrives on fresh herbs—mint or basil are particularly good.

Substituting orange zest and juice for the lemon makes a perfect complement to these dishes. You could also prepare a little crust for the fish by combining a few tablespoons of gremolata and ½ cup (50 g) of bread crumbs. Mix them together in a small bowl and coat the fish on both sides prior to baking. It will create a lovely crunchy golden crumb around the outside of the fish. You can then add the remaining fresh gremolata over the top.

There are numerous types of fish you can use for this tasty dish. Make sure you choose a firm, fleshy fish such as salmon or halibut. These types of fish retain their shape well during preparation and cooking. You can use frozen seafood, although it does lose its flavor a little, which is why I always use fresh when possible.

To turn this into a one-tray meal, add some diced potatoes, which will absorb the flavors of the fish and tomatoes. Potatoes will take longer to cook, so give them a head start by placing them in the oven 35 minutes before adding the fish and tomatoes. Move the potatoes to the sides of the baking dish, place the cod in the center and the tomatoes over the potatoes.

Gremolata

1 cup (60 g) finely chopped flat-leaf parsley

3 cloves garlic, peeled and finely minced

Zest and juice of 1 lemon

½ cup (120 ml) extra virgin olive oil

Salt

Cod

1 lb (454 g) cod, salmon or halibut fillets

1¼ cups (190 g) mixed cherry tomatoes, cut in half

2 tbsp (30 ml) extra virgin olive oil

Salt and freshly ground black pepper

Method

To make the gremolata: Put the parsley, garlic, lemon zest and juice and olive oil into a food processor and pulse until roughly chopped, adding a little more lemon juice or salt according to taste. If you don't have a food processor, finely chop your parsley and garlic, add to a bowl with the lemon zest and juice and olive oil and mix together very well. Feel free to add some fresh chile or dried red pepper flakes for some heat.

To make the cod: Preheat the oven to 350°F (175°C). Place the fish in the center of a 13 x 9–inch (33 x 23–cm) baking dish, and scatter the cherry tomatoes around it. Adding baby potatoes to the dish will make it a heartier meal. For crisper potatoes, parboil them for 8 to 10 minutes, drain and add them to the baking dish; they will absorb the flavors of the fish.

Add the olive oil, and season well with salt and pepper. Put the dish into the oven and bake for 20 to 25 minutes, until the cod is cooked through and the tomatoes are blistered. Serve the cod surrounded by the tomatoes on a large platter and topped with the gremolata.

Baked Chicken Drumsticks

These baked chicken drumsticks are super succulent and utterly delicious. Peppers and carrots offer a lovely sweetness to the seasoned chicken. Chicken is quite commonly used in Italian cuisine, whether it's baked, stewed or fried; these recipes are very popular and are kept in the family for years.

Using good-quality chicken drumsticks is key—and they are very affordable. I use them a lot when making a chicken broth or stock, as the flavor in the meat and bone are incredible. Alternatively, you can use bone-in chicken thighs or wings. I try to steer clear of using chicken breasts in this recipe as they can dry out quite quickly in the oven.

This dish has very few ingredients, so make sure you season the chicken really well. During the cooking process, the juice from the chicken collects in the dish and creates a sauce that tastes amazing when mopped up with some fresh ciabatta. You can also play around with different vegetables—1 or 2 medium-sized potatoes, sweet potatoes or parsnips are great options, as they will withstand the long cooking time. You can most definitely add sliced zucchini or eggplant, but they offer a slightly different taste and can make the dish extra watery. It's best to add these types of vegetables toward the last 15 to 20 minutes of cooking, so they retain their shape. For a salty bite, ½ cup (90 g) of pitted black olives does the trick. Add them in with the chicken, carrot, onion and bell pepper.

I like the combination of fresh herbs like the ones listed in this recipe. The rosemary and oregano are the perfect combo for baked chicken, as they have a wonderful woody flavor. For something more savory, substitute a combination of fresh sage and thyme. You can also grate the zest of a lemon into the mix for a tangy citrus twist.

Ingredients

2 lb (1 kg) chicken drumsticks, skin on

1 tsp fresh oregano leaves

1 sprig of rosemary, stem removed and leaves roughly chopped

Salt and freshly ground black pepper

2 cloves garlic, finely sliced

1 white onion, peeled and cut into quarters

1 large carrot, peeled and sliced lengthwise

1 small green or red bell pepper, cored, seeded and sliced into strips

1 (14-oz [400-g]) can diced tomatoes

2 tbsp (30 g) cold butter, diced

2 tbsp (30 ml) extra virgin olive oil

Method

Preheat the oven to 350°F (175°C). Lay the chicken drumsticks in a 13 x 9–inch (33 x 23–cm) baking dish and season really well with your choice of herbs. Add the oregano, rosemary and a generous amount of salt and pepper.

Scatter the garlic, onion, carrot and bell pepper around the chicken and pour the tomatoes over. Put the diced butter on the chicken, and drizzle the olive oil all over. Use a spoon to stir well. The most important thing is to cover the dish with parchment paper and secure it tightly with foil. This will allow the chicken to cook evenly without any of the heat escaping, keeping it moist and succulent.

Put the dish into the oven to bake. After 30 minutes, uncover, turn the chicken legs over and stir. Cover it back up and cook for another 30 minutes. The vegetables will break down with the juices, creating a lovely sauce. You can remove the foil for the last 10 to 15 minutes of baking, if you'd like, which allows the chicken to turn a little golden and the sauce to thicken up.

Serve the drumsticks in the baking dish or on a large platter and pour all the juices from the dish directly over them.

Fritto Misto di Mare

This dish is the Italian version of fish and chips! Fritto misto is a combination of fish fried in a light coating of batter and served in brown paper cones. Trust me when I say that this is the ultimate take-out dish. I spent some time in Sorrento on the Amalfi Coast, and I ate one of the most marvelous plates of fritto misto at sunset right on the beach.

Fritto Misto di Mare consists of assorted seafood, such as shrimp, sardines, anchovy fillets, snapper, calamari and so many others. Italians like to use the freshest locally caught seafood available to make this well-known dish. For fritto misto, you want fish that tastes great and holds its shape when frying. Snapper, cod and swordfish are great choices, and baby octopus, calamari and shrimp provide variety of flavors and textures.

It's best to keep smaller fish (sardines, anchovies) whole, but larger fish can be cut into bite-sized pieces. Be creative with your choice of seafood. The taste of fritto misto heavily relies on the freshness of the seafood, the batter and seasoning. Adding ½ teaspoon of chile powder and ½ teaspoon of garlic powder to the batter is an excellent way to spice things up.

It all begins with a good-quality batter. Many recipes call for all-purpose flour, but I like to use semolina. Semolina has a finer, grainier texture, so when fried it provides a crunch that all-purpose doesn't. You can create the same effect with fine polenta, but the taste will be slightly different, as polenta is a corn grain. Using a mixture of semolina and rice flour helps give the fried seafood an extra-crispy layer. If neither of these two options is available, then all-purpose flour will work, but it may create a heavier batter. Remember to shake off the excess batter before frying. Using a carbonated liquid such as soda water or sparkling water works as a leavening agent which helps to keep the batter light and airy.

The batter suggested is not just strictly for seafood. It is perfect for vegetables too. Stick to vegetables that retain their shape when frying: thin pumpkin slices, baby broccoli, carrots, zucchini, green beans, cauliflower and fennel quarters. The thicker vegetables will take a little longer to fry, about 3 to 4 minutes, so keep on checking them for your preferred texture.

Seafood

½ lb (226 g) firm white fish, such as cod or snapper, cleaned and cut into 1½-inch (4-cm) pieces

½ lb (226 g) whitebait

½ lb (226 g) calamari

½ lb (226 g) prawns or shrimp, cleaned and deveined, with tails intact

Batter

½ cup (110 g) semolina flour or polenta/cornmeal

½ cup (110 g) rice flour

1¼ cups (300 ml) soda water, chilled

Vegetable oil, for frying

Salt and freshly ground black pepper

3 lemons, sliced into wedges, for serving

Method

You can clean the seafood yourself or ask your fish seller to do it for you. Pat it all dry with a paper towel.

To make the batter: In a large mixing bowl, add the semolina (or polenta/cornmeal), rice flour and soda water. Whisk gently to create a smooth and creamy batter. You want to create a batter that is light enough to coat the fish. If the batter seems a little thick, add a little more liquid to loosen it up. Use the quantities above at your discretion to create your desired thickness.

Fill a pot or deep fryer halfway with vegetable oil and heat until it reaches 400°F (200°C). Test the heat by pouring a little of the batter into the hot oil. It will rise quickly to the surface when the oil is ready. Dip the pieces of fish into the batter one by one, starting with the thickest cuts of seafood, as they will take a little longer to cook than prawns or whitebait. Tap off any excess batter before carefully placing the battered seafood into the hot oil. Fry for about 2 to 3 minutes, until golden. Gauge how many pieces will fit in your fryer, because you don't want to overcrowd your fryer with too many at once. The same timing applies if you're frying vegetables. Start with the harder veggies, working your way down to the softer ones.

Remove the seafood or vegetables from the oil with a slotted spoon and drain on paper towels. Season generously with salt and pepper and squeeze the juice of a lemon wedge or two over the top.

Serve the Fritto Misto di Mare in handmade parchment cones or brown paper serving bags with the remaining lemon wedges.

Saltimbocca alla Romana

Loosely translated as "jump in the mouth," *saltimbocca* is a satisfying and simple dish that will wow the guests at your next dinner party. It originates from Brescia, a large city in the Lombardy region. The Romans took ownership of the dish and renamed it.

Saltimbocca alla Romana's flavor is elevated by the combination of the buttery sauce, the salty prosciutto and thin, tender veal scallops (*escalopes* in French). The hero of the dish of course is the veal, and the trick is to get it nice and tender prior to frying. Each piece of veal should be roughly ¼ inch (6 mm) thick. Placing each piece in between two pieces of parchment paper and pounding it with a meat mallet to achieve the same thickness will ensure that the meat is tenderized and will cook evenly and stay moist.

Chicken or pork partner well with the saltiness of the prosciutto. I recommend using 1 pound (454 g) of boneless, skinless, thinly cut chicken breast. If the prosciutto crudo is too salty, you can use 6 thin slices of smoked ham.

Boneless pork loin or pork loin steaks can be substituted for the veal as well. I've used white wine in this recipe, which adds a crisp taste to the sauce. You can also use red wine, Marsala, Madeira or sherry. If you prefer not to include alcohol in this dish, a little chicken stock or water can be used as a wonderful alternative.

Ingredients

6 veal scallops

6 thin slices of prosciutto crudo

6 fresh sage leaves, plus more for serving

Salt and freshly ground black pepper

¼ cup (30 g) all-purpose flour

¼ cup (60 ml) extra virgin olive oil

¼ cup (60 ml) dry white wine or Marsala

¼ cup (60 g) unsalted butter

Method

Place the veal between two pieces of parchment paper and pound it with a meat mallet until it's ¼ inch (6 mm) thick. This helps to break down the meat's fibers and tenderizes it, which aids the cooking process. I recommend the same ¼-inch (6-mm) thickness for chicken or pork.

Working with 1 slice of prosciutto or ham at a time, place it in the center of the veal followed by a fresh sage leaf. If the sage leaves are on the smaller size, use two for each piece of veal. Secure it with one or two wooden toothpicks. Season lightly with a little salt and a generous amount of pepper. Put the flour into a shallow bowl, and lightly coat the veal parcels, dusting off any excess. Repeat until all the scallops have been coated.

Heat a large saucepan over low-to-medium heat with the olive oil. Cook the veal two or three pieces at a time for about 1 to 2 minutes on each side, until slightly crispy and brown. Since they are very thin cuts of meat, keep an eye on them, as they will cook very quickly. After browning, transfer to a plate and set aside.

Deglaze the pan with the wine, scraping up the brown bits that have stuck to the bottom. Stir in the butter, and once it has started to melt, return all the veal to the pan and cook for another 2 to 3 minutes, until the sauce thickens and becomes glossy. If you love sage like I do, add a few leaves in when you melt the butter, as they will give the sauce a slightly peppery taste.

Serve your Saltimbocca alla Romana on a platter, with the sauce poured all over the meat, alongside my Buttery Parmesan-Roasted Potatoes (page 140).

Chapter Five

A Beautiful Beginning

Antipasto means "before the meal," and no respectable Italian meal would begin without it. We start our meals with something to tantalize the taste buds before the pasta or primi course comes out. Antipasto dishes are light and full of color and flavor. The combination of cured meats, preserved or pickled vegetables and cheeses varies from region to region.

The northern regions primarily focus on lighter fare, such as creamy cheeses, fresh fish, polenta and bright, fragrant pesto. The southern regions focus more on bold, striking flavors, including rich tomatoes, fiery sopressata, hard cheeses and salty capers and anchovies.

No antipasto is complete without a stunning focaccia. My Anchovy & Rosemary Oil Focaccia with Olives (page 122) is an excellent one to start with. My Roasted Fig & Burrata Crostini (page 126) can be tailored to your personal taste by creating your own stunning toppings.

Every now and again I really enjoy eating antipasto dishes as my main meal. There is so much variety, as they come in almost bite-sized portions, which means you can have a little of everything. During the summer I eat these types of dishes at almost every meal.

Fresh & Simple Bruschetta

In this famous Italian staple, the classic combination of plump, ripe tomatoes and fresh basil comes together to create the ever-so-simple starter we all know and love. Bruschetta is derived from the word *bruscare*, which means "to roast over coals" in the Roman dialect. The bread is grilled and rubbed with fresh garlic, which is then topped with fresh tomatoes, herbs and salt. It's another simple dish that can be easily altered to suit your tastes and style.

It's essential to use the best extra virgin olive oil you can get. Since there are very few ingredients, each needs to stand out. Bruschetta calls for fresh garlic, but since this is a very strong ingredient, it could be reduced or left out altogether. I strongly advise not using garlic powder as this can take away from the freshness of the dish. Substituting different fresh herbs, such as 1 tablespoon (2 g) of oregano or thyme leaves, is also a way to change up the flavors. Fresh herbs are best in bruschetta, but you can also use dried herbs if you have them on hand, although the flavors may not be as dramatic.

You want to make sure the tomatoes retain their firmness, so avoid adding salt to the mixture while it is marinating in the refrigerator. Salt will draw out all the moisture and will leave the tomatoes mushy. It is always best to season the tomatoes just prior to serving.

Before you serve the bruschetta, feel free to top it with either an 8-ounce (226-g) ball of fresh mozzarella or the same amount of fresh bocconcini. For a saltier bruschetta, top the tomatoes with 1 tablespoon (7 g) of capers, ½ cup (90 g) of marinated mixed olives or 6 to 8 anchovy fillets.

Instead of a traditional tomato version, try a sweeter option with 1 cup (150 g) of roasted red grapes and sweet, spreadable ricotta. Or, add 2 tablespoons (40 g) of Nutella, topped with mixed berries and fresh mint. This sweet version is perfect for a quick and easy dessert. Let your imagination run wild!

Ingredients

8 firm, ripe plum tomatoes

⅔ cup (160 ml) extra virgin olive oil, divided

2 cloves garlic, minced

1 fresh baguette, sliced diagonally into ½-inch (1.3-cm) pieces

1 clove garlic, whole

A large handful of fresh basil leaves, roughly torn

Salt and freshly ground black pepper

Method

Rinse the tomatoes. Dry them with a tea towel and roughly chop. This is a fairly rustic dish, so it is really up to you on how big or small you would like the size of your tomatoes. Put the chopped tomatoes in a bowl and coat with ⅓ cup (80 ml) of the olive oil and the minced garlic, then mix well. Allow the mixture to marinate for 15 minutes so the flavors can combine.

If you are using dried herbs such as oregano or thyme, add these in while the tomatoes are marinating to help intensify the flavor. You could add the basil leaves or any other fresh herb at this point, but I find they lose their color and freshness, so I like to add them at the end.

Prepare any ingredients you plan to add, such as mozzarella, bocconcini, capers or anchovies while the tomatoes are marinating. I recommend tossing in these ingredients or laying them over the tops of the bruschetta just prior to serving.

Toast the baguette slices on a hot grill pan. Flip over so both sides are golden brown, and set aside. Slice the whole garlic clove in half and rub it on one side of each of the slices of toast. I love to use this method, as it perfectly coats the bread, infusing it with garlic flavor. The more garlic the better, I say!

To serve, arrange the slices of toasted bread on a large platter, spooning the marinated tomatoes onto each one of the slices. Scatter the basil or your choice of herbs over the top, drizzle with the remaining ⅓ cup (80 ml) of olive oil and season with salt and a little pepper. *Magnifico!*

Prosciutto & Melon Salad with Homemade Basil Oil

The words *prosciutto e melone* scream Italian summer. This dish is iconic for a reason: It's the perfect combination of bright colors and balance of sweetness and salt. Since it contains only a few ingredients, use the best-quality produce, meat and cheese you can find. The duo of prosciutto and melon represents Italian cuisine at its best.

Make sure the melon is ripe and sweet and that your prosciutto is very thinly sliced. Fruit is a fairly easy ingredient to pair with prosciutto, as the sweet flavor balances the saltiness of the meat. I have made this recipe before using different types of melons, including honeydew and watermelon. These two are perfect if you wish to change up the flavor.

In the warmer months, when stone fruit is in season, use peaches, plums or apricots, which work extremely well with the meat. Slice about 1 cup (226 g) of fruit, arrange the slices on a large platter and add the other ingredients. Prosciutto is the second hero of this dish, but if prosciutto is not available, try 12 to 15 slices of capocollo or salami. They bring the same saltness as the prosciutto. If you prefer less salt, substitute thinly sliced ham. It has a sweet, smoky taste that is not overpowering.

I've paired this dish with my basil oil, which really brightens it up. If you want to keep it simple, feel free to use 3 tablespoons (45 ml) of extra virgin olive oil instead, which you can lightly drizzle over the top. I absolutely enjoy eating this dish all the time, especially during the summer months, when it is too hot to cook and I want something fresh and light.

Homemade Basil Oil

1 cup (24 g) fresh basil leaves, stems removed

½ cup (120 ml) extra virgin olive oil

1 tsp dried red pepper flakes

2 cloves garlic, halved

2 tsp (12 g) salt

Salad

1 cantaloupe

14 thin slices prosciutto di Parma

12 oz (340 g) fresh mozzarella or baby bocconcini cheese

A handful of fresh basil leaves, roughly torn

Method

To make the basil oil: Put the basil leaves in a food processor. Add the olive oil, red pepper flakes, garlic and salt. Pulse until the ingredients are just combined. I like to keep the basil oil fairly rustic with larger bits of leaves, but pulse until you get the desired consistency.

To make the salad: Slice the melon in half and use a spoon to remove the seeds from the center. Cut lengthwise into 1-inch (2.5-cm) slices, and remove the rind. If you are using stone fruit, make sure you rinse each piece well and remove the pit from each center, then slice into halves or quarters.

Wrap a fresh piece of prosciutto, or your choice of cured meat, around each slice of fruit, keeping it relatively loose. Arrange each piece onto a large platter, repeating until all ingredients have been used.

I love using torn pieces of fresh mozzarella or halved baby bocconcini nestled into each of the wrapped parcels. If you want to add a creamier cheese, ricotta works perfectly. Drizzle a few large tablespoons (30 ml) of the homemade basil oil (or olive oil) over the top of the salad, and scatter fresh basil leaves between each of the slices.

Serve the Prosciutto & Melon Salad with Homemade Basil Oil on a hot summer night for a light and tasty meal.

Classic Beef Carpaccio

Beef carpaccio is fresh and light and takes minimum effort to make. Yes, it is raw meat, but when sliced paper thin, it's an elegant starter to any meal. It is said this dish is named after Vittore Carpaccio, a 15th-century Venetian painter who used lots of red and white in his work. Giuseppe Cipriani, the owner of Harry's Bar in Venice, created this dish in the 1950s, and it has been popular ever since.

Carpaccio is traditionally made with high-quality beef fillet sliced extremely thin and topped with a creamy sauce. The salty fried capers and the acid of the lemon combine to elevate the taste. Understandably, beef carpaccio is not for everyone, but when it's prepared properly with the freshest, highest-quality ingredients, it is hard to resist.

If beef is not your first preference, it can be replaced with 1 pound (454 g) of thinly sliced smoked salmon or fresh tuna fillet, which can be served with a little dill, arugula and a zesty lemon oil. To make a vegetarian carpaccio, thinly slice 1 or 2 large zucchini or carrots lengthwise and serve with some fresh herbs, such as 2 tablespoons (about 9 g) of mint or parsley, and a generous drizzle of extra virgin olive oil.

Carpaccio is served with olive oil, capers, lemon juice and shaved Parmesan cheese. The sauce is a light mayonnaise, which is drizzled over the beef and is a wonderful complement to the meat.

Beef Carpaccio	Sauce
1 lb (454 g) beef fillet, thinly sliced	1 egg yolk
2 tbsp (30 ml) extra virgin olive oil, divided	2 tbsp (30 g) Dijon mustard
2 tbsp (15 g) capers, drained	1–2 tsp (5–10 ml) fresh lemon juice
2 handfuls fresh arugula leaves	2 tbsp (30 ml) extra virgin olive oil, divided
Salt and freshly ground black pepper	2 tbsp (30 ml) whole milk or heavy cream
3 oz (80 g) shaved Parmesan cheese	Salt to and freshly ground pepper
1 lemon, sliced into wedges	

Method

First and foremost, the beef, or other protein, needs to be prepared prior to slicing. Wrap the beef fillet, salmon or tuna tightly in plastic wrap and put in either the refrigerator for 2 hours or the freezer for 25 to 30 minutes. Partially freezing the protein and using a very sharp knife will ensure that when you slice into it, you will achieve very thin slices of meat. This step is essential when making carpaccio, as anything slightly thicker will not have the same texture or taste. If you are using vegetables, there is no need to freeze. Peel and slice them thinly using a knife or a mandoline to achieve the desired thickness.

While the beef is in the refrigerator, make the sauce. In a small bowl, whisk the egg yolk, Dijon mustard and lemon juice until combined. While whisking, slowly pour in 1 tablespoon plus 1 teaspoon (20 ml) of the olive oil until the mixture thickens. Stir in the milk or cream and season well with salt and pepper. You can add this mustard sauce to salmon or tuna carpaccio or for a much lighter sauce, you can combine olive oil, dill, lemon juice and salt and pepper. Cover and place in the refrigerator until the meat is ready to be sliced.

In a small saucepan over medium heat, add a tablespoon (15 ml) of olive oil and fry the capers for 1 to 2 minutes, until lightly crispy. Remove with a slotted spoon and drain well on paper towels. In a large bowl, add the arugula, salt and pepper and the other 1 tablespoon (15 ml) of olive oil. Toss gently to combine and set aside.

Remove the plastic wrap from the beef, and put the meat onto a clean cutting board. Use a very sharp knife to carefully slice the meat into wafer-thin pieces. Layer the beef, tuna or salmon slices on the base of a large platter or serving board. Scatter the fried capers, arugula salad and shaved Parmesan cheese over the meat. Squeeze some fresh lemon juice and drizzle the remaining 2 teaspoons (10 ml) of olive oil over the top of the sliced meat. I love to drizzle the mustard sauce all over the beef carpaccio, but you can serve this on the side for everyone to help themselves.

Anchovy & Rosemary Oil Focaccia with Olives

Focaccia is a delicious Italian bread that has a similar baking style to pizza, although there are a few key differences. It's most commonly made with traditional ingredients such as olive oil, sea salt and rosemary, but today you can put almost anything onto a focaccia.

Over the years I have seen so many different takes on the classic focaccia and have been mesmerized by the trend of focaccia art. This is created by making gorgeous designs on the surface of the bread with fresh vegetables and herbs. Focaccia can be served cold and makes an excellent starter to any meal.

The olives and anchovies can be substituted with a variety of other ingredients. You can use 1 cup (100 g) of homemade Pepe Arrostiti (page 22) scattered all over the base of the dough to create a peppery, smoky-tasting focaccia. Or, you can top the focaccia with the caramelized onions from the pizza chapter (page 79). Stick to 1-cup (100-g) quantities of alternative ingredients, or add more if you prefer. Try some sautéed mushrooms and fresh tomato slices layered over the top. Two tablespoons (15 g) of capers with the sliced tomatoes is a match made in heaven.

You could also make a sweet version using red grapes, mixed berries or peaches, depending on the season. I recommend using stone fruit or berries for focaccia, but pear or apple slices would work well too. Dried rosemary or thyme pair well with stone fruit such as peaches, plums or nectarines, and you can also enhance the sweetness of the fruit by drizzling 1 to 2 tablespoons (15 to 30 ml) of honey over it.

The possibilities are endless, so feel free to experiment with different flavor combinations and adjust according to your tastes.

Anchovy & Rosemary Oil

½ cup (120 ml) extra virgin olive oil

2 cloves garlic, sliced

3 tbsp (15 g) fresh rosemary leaves, roughly chopped

10–12 whole anchovy fillets

Focaccia

1 cup (240 ml) warm water

1 tbsp (15 g) granulated sugar

2 tsp (7 g) dried yeast

2½ cups (315 g) all-purpose flour

½ cup (90 g) marinated Kalamata olives, pitted and roughly chopped

Salt, for serving

Method

You can make the anchovy and rosemary oil well ahead of time and store it prior to use. If you are making a sweet focaccia with stone fruit, you can skip ahead and make the dough.

To make the anchovy and rosemary oil: In a small saucepan over low heat, add the olive oil, garlic, rosemary and anchovies and stir to combine. Heat the oil so the anchovies melt slightly into it, allowing the flavors to come together. The longer the flavors sit, the more intense they will become. Once heated, pour the oil mixture into a jar to cool, and set aside.

To make the focaccia: In a small bowl, whisk together the water, sugar and yeast. Set aside for 10 minutes to allow the yeast to proof. The surface will become foamy when it's ready to use. In a large bowl, add the flour, Kalamata olives, ¼ cup (60 ml) of the rosemary and anchovy oil and the yeast mixture. Use your hands to bring the ingredients together to make a soft dough. Knead the dough for a few minutes, until smooth. If you'd like, you may oil the bowl with 1 tablespoon (15 ml) of the anchovy and rosemary oil to coat the dough and prevent sticking. However, I don't find this is usually necessary because there is already oil in the dough. Keep the dough in the bowl, cover with a damp tea towel and set aside in a dark place at room temperature for about an hour, or until it doubles in size.

Coat the sides and bottom of a 1-quart (900-ml) oval baking dish with a little of the anchovy and rosemary oil. I find using a deep dish will really help give the focaccia its thickness. Carefully transfer the dough to the oiled dish and use your palms to carefully push and stretch out the dough to the ends of the pan. Cover once again with a damp tea towel and put in a dark place for another 1 hour, until it doubles in size.

Preheat the oven to 350°F (175°C). Use your fingertips to create little dimples all over the surface of the dough. Pour the remaining anchovy and rosemary oil over the top of the focaccia. Italian cooking is all about the experience, so it doesn't need to be perfect. The more rustic, the better! Try adding some sliced cherry tomatoes pressed into the dough with some fresh rosemary, or keep it simple with some minced garlic and oregano leaves. If you're making a sweet version, arrange the fruit or mixed berries all over the base of the dough, using the herbs you prefer.

Bake for 20 to 25 minutes, until golden brown. Remove it from the oven, keeping it in the baking dish and allowing it to cool completely before slicing. Serve the focaccia with a light sprinkle of salt and an array of cured meats and pickled vegetables.

Gnocchi Fritto with Cured Meats & Cheeses

Gnocchi fritto is a delicious bite-sized appetizer that is found in most bars and restaurants in Italy. Created in Emilia-Romagna, these soft, puffy pillows of goodness are accompanied by cured meats and cheeses. It's no wonder they are a hit.

I have seen many recipes use water instead of milk or a combination of the two. Personally, I like to use whole milk rather than water, as I feel it gives the dough a little sweetness. You can use ¼ cup (60 ml) of milk and ¼ cup (60 ml) of water, or ½ cup (120 ml) of water to keep it fairly simple.

I use Tipo 00 flour, as it's the absolute gold standard in Italian cooking. It is a much finer flour, which helps the gnocchi fritto to fry quickly and come out much lighter. Tipo 00 flour can be found at various grocery stores, but if it's not available, all-purpose flour will do the job. An excellent tip when making gnocchi fritto is to make sure to roll out the pieces of dough relatively thin prior to cutting.

Back in the day, gnocchi fritto were fried in lard (pork fat). Over the years it has been adapted, and now most people use vegetable oil or sunflower oil, as I have done in this recipe.

You can also create a sweeter option by adding 1 to 2 tablespoons (15 to 30 ml) of honey to the dough. Once fried, dust them with a generous amount of confectioners' sugar, and serve these with fresh berries and Nutella.

The shape of your gnocchi is completely up to you. Italians like to leave nothing to waste, so any leftover pieces of dough can be fried and eaten. I use a ravioli cutter, as I like the crinkled edges, although using a regular knife is absolutely fine to create your desired shape.

Ingredients

½ cup (120 ml) whole milk

2 tbsp (7 g) active dry yeast

1¾ cups (220 g) Tipo 00 flour or all-purpose flour

2 tsp (30 g) vegetable shortening or soft butter

1 tsp granulated sugar

½ tsp salt

4 cups (1 L) vegetable oil, for frying

Method

Heat the milk in a saucepan until lukewarm and sprinkle the yeast over the top. If using only water, make sure you use warm water to proof the yeast. Whisk the mixture and allow it to sit for 10 minutes, until foamy.

Working on a clean surface, combine the flour, vegetable shortening, sugar and salt, and use your hand to make a well in the center of the mixture. If you are making the dessert option, add a few tablespoons (about 30 ml) of honey. Pour the milk or water into the flour well and use your hands to bring the dough together.

Knead the dough for 10 minutes, until smooth and stretchy. If the dough feels sticky, add a few handfuls of flour to prevent it from sticking to the surface. If you prefer, you can also make the dough in a stand mixer with a dough hook attachment. Transfer the dough to a large bowl, cover in plastic wrap and set it aside in a dark place for 2 hours, or until it has doubled in size.

Once the dough has risen, cut it into four pieces, and, working with one piece at a time, roll out the dough as thin as you can. You can use some elbow grease and a rolling pin, but a pasta machine will speed up the process.

The pasta machine will create a perfectly even thinness on all your rolled pieces of dough. Cover the remaining pieces of dough with a damp tea towel to prevent them from drying out.

Use a ravioli cutter or knife to cut the gnocchi into the shapes you want. You can keep it fairly simple by cutting the dough into squares, diamonds or rectangles. Put them onto a lightly floured baking sheet until you have used up all the dough and are ready to fry them.

In a large, deep saucepan, heat the oil to 350°F (175°C). Working quickly, fry the pieces of dough in batches, about five or six at a time. They are very thin, so they will fry extremely fast. You'll know they're done when they puff up and turn golden brown on both sides. Use a slotted spoon and transfer them to a paper towel to drain. Continue working in batches until all the dough has been fried.

Serve warm alongside cured meats and a creamy cheese such as stracchino. If you have made dessert gnocchi, dust them with a generous amount of confectioners' sugar and serve with Nutella and fresh fruit, such as mixed berries or sliced bananas.

Roasted Fig & Burrata Crostini

Crostini are found all over Italy but more commonly in the northern regions, such as Umbria and Venice. Since there are so many alternatives you can create, crostini are made all year long using whatever foods are in season.

It is said that crostini (along with bruschetta) originated in medieval times. Since serveware was a luxury, peasants would have their meals on stale pieces of bread. Crostini are simple but decadent, brushed with extra virgin olive oil and topped with meat, fish, cheese and seasonal vegetables or fruits.

Roasted figs and creamy burrata is one of my favorite combinations. You can create other flavor combinations with fresh mozzarella, some Pepe Arrostiti (page 22) and 1 tablespoon (3 g) of dried oregano. Or, try roasting 1 cup (150 g) of red seedless grapes and add them to toasted bread with some ricotta and rosemary. Add some cream cheese topped with smoked salmon and dill for an elegant-looking crostini, or perhaps go Mediterranean with mixed olives and sun-dried tomatoes over some ricotta. Keep your ingredients fresh, light, and seasonal.

You can use a baguette as I have in this recipe, for the perfect bite-sized shape for the toasts, but this is also a great way to use fresh bread if you prefer or have some on hand. Make my Rustic Italian Bread (page 42), and cut thick slices into halves, squares or triangles, then toast and add the toppings. If you are entertaining, you can even make the elements a few days in advance along with the toppings, and assemble everything right before your guests arrive. They are quick and simple to prepare, making them an excellent finger-food starter.

Ingredients

10 fresh figs, stems removed and cut into quarters

¼ cup (60 ml) honey

1 baguette, cut diagonally into 1½-inch (4-cm)-thick slices

¼ cup (60 ml) extra virgin olive oil, for brushing

8 oz (226 g) fresh burrata cheese

A handful of fresh arugula

Method

Preheat the oven to 350°F (175°C) and prepare an 8 x 8–inch (20 x 20–cm) baking dish to roast the figs. Place the figs into the baking dish. Drizzle the honey evenly over the top of the fruit and put in the oven.

Roast for 15 to 20 minutes, until the figs are soft and have caramelized. If you're using grapes, rinse them and remove the stems prior to roasting. Some great alternatives include roasted strawberries drizzled with a little vanilla, sliced pears or a mixture of fresh berries. I recommend adding juicy fruits just before serving so the bread doesn't become soggy.

Brush both sides of each slice of bread with a little olive oil and heat on a grill pan until the bread is golden brown. Keep an eye on the bread, as it can burn quickly. If you don't have a grill pan, toast the bread in a frying pan on the stove top or in the oven or toaster to achieve the same golden-brown color.

Spread a generous amount of burrata on one side of the bread and place a few arugula leaves on top. Feel free to use ricotta or feta as a substitute for the burrata. Place a few of the caramelized figs, or your choice of roasted fruit, on the top of the arugula and spoon a little of the honey from the baking dish over each of the crostini.

For a savory twist, add some torn mozzarella with my homemade Pepe Arrostiti (page 22) over the top with a sprinkle of fresh rosemary. Serve on a large platter or cutting board along with a Negroni or Spritz Veneziano.

Chapter Six

Fresh & Vibrant Sides

Vegetables can be used in almost anything when it comes to Italian cooking. It is no secret that the Italians treat their vegetables with respect and love. In order to have seasonal vegetables all year long, they tend and care for their homegrown loves like they would their own children. If you don't believe me, just ask any Italian with a vegetable patch in their backyard.

Whether they are baked, roasted, braised or stuffed, vegetables are the essence of Mediterranean cooking. They are added to almost everything, from pasta to pizza, and are absolutely perfect on their own. I love roasting vegetables, as it deepens their natural flavors. Good-quality olive oil and fresh herbs and spices help the vegetables to shine even brighter.

The following recipes are some of my family's favorites and are very adaptable, so anyone can create a new favorite in the kitchen. Pomodori Ripieni (page 138) can be made with tomatoes or sweet bell peppers. Panzanella (page 132) is kept simple but can be elevated with salty capers and olives. These sides are colorful and flavorful and they invite in many new tastes and textures.

Crispy Cauliflower Fritters

Simple and delicious, these cauliflower fritters are the perfect bite-sized side dish. I find that cauliflower doesn't get the credit it deserves. It is a versatile ingredient that can be served on its own simply prepared with some salty grated Parmesan cheese and parsley, which is how I love to make it.

You can use what you have on hand, especially those leftover vegetables, to make all kinds of fritters. Traditionally, the batter is made up of flour, eggs and garlic, and you can add alternative ingredients from there. Start with a star vegetable, such as the cauliflower used in this recipe, or 1 head of broccoli. A large sweet potato or zucchini would also work well.

The aim is to keep the cauliflower roughly in its shape, as you want the pieces to be quite chunky when combining them with the batter. My nonna's trick is to put the boiled cauliflower into a large bowl filled with cold water. This helps to stop the cooking process and prevent the cauliflower from becoming mushy.

You could repeat this process if using alternate ingredients such as broccoli. If using vegetables such as grated zucchini or sweet potato, add it straight into the batter. Zucchini retains a lot of water, so remember to squeeze out the liquid after it's grated. Basil leaves and some lemon zest will give the fritter a burst of brightness. Try scallions, baby spinach or Swiss chard. I've added a mix of pecorino and Parmesan, as I really enjoy the combination of the two, although you could try cheddar for a different taste. Stick to hard cheeses, as they help keep the fritters intact during frying.

Ingredients

1 head cauliflower, stem removed, cut into bite-sized florets

½ cup (63 g) all-purpose flour

½ cup (50 g) grated Parmesan cheese

½ cup (50 g) grated pecorino cheese

3 eggs, lightly beaten

3 cloves garlic, minced

3 tbsp (11 g) chopped flat-leaf parsley

Salt and freshly ground black pepper

Olive oil, for frying

Method

Fill a large pot with water and bring it to a boil. Add a little salt and the cauliflower or broccoli florets and boil for 8 minutes, until tender. Drain the cauliflower or broccoli and allow to cool completely. Alternatively, grate 1 large sweet potato or zucchini. Remember to squeeze out any excess liquid from the zucchini.

Squeeze out any excess liquid from the cauliflower. Doing this will help the florets to bind well with the other ingredients. Put the cauliflower, or other veggies, into a large bowl and add the flour, Parmesan, pecorino, eggs, garlic and parsley, and season with salt and pepper. Mix until all the ingredients are combined. Mix in any other herbs and spices, if desired, at this point. If the mixture seems a little dry, add a few tablespoons (30 ml) of water to loosen it up. If the mixture is too wet, add a few tablespoons (16 g) of flour or (13 g) of Parmesan to thicken it. The mixture should be soft and wet, but not too runny. When you add a tablespoon (15 ml) full of batter to the hot oil, you want the mixture to stay together.

In a large saucepan, pour in enough oil to cover the base of the frying pan. Heat the oil over medium heat. Use a tablespoon to form the mixture into little fritters and place them into the hot oil. Press down gently on the fritter with a spatula to flatten them slightly.

Cook the fritters in batches to prevent them from sticking to one another, about 3 to 4 minutes per side. Flip them over using a fork and gently press down, making sure they retain their shape. Remove them from the pan once they're golden on both sides, and transfer them to a plate lined with a paper towel to soak up the excess oil. If you would like a lighter option, try baking them in the oven at 350°F (175°C) for 25 to 30 minutes, until they are golden brown. They will not have those crispy outer edges that you get with deep frying, but they will be equally delicious.

Serve immediately alongside Roasted Mediterranean Vegetables (page 134) or Baked Chicken Drumsticks (page 108).

Panzanella

A traditional panzanella is made up of very simple ingredients that many Italians have growing in their gardens. I love making this salad, as it reminds me of warm summer days spent in the Italian countryside.

This salad originated in Tuscany and is found all over Italy—with each region adapting it to their own unique style. You can make this salad in the traditional way or be as adventurous as you like. Keep it colorful and balanced as far as acidity and saltiness go.

Stale bread is usually used in this dish, so please don't discard any you have lying around. Italians like to make use of everything! A rustic loaf with a crunchy crust works best, so use ciabatta, like I have, or sourdough. Toasting the bread adds a golden tone and extra crunch to the salad.

Ripe, fresh tomatoes are key for a panzanella. When sliced, the tomato juice will run to the bottom of the bowl and serve as the base of your dressing. Heirloom tomatoes, if they are in season, work wonderfully along with a mix of cherry tomatoes.

Feel free to add whatever you like to this salad. I've used a cucumber for an added burst of freshness, but you could also add 1 tablespoon (15 g) of capers or 2 red bell peppers diced into small cubes. Anchovies can also be used, so depending on your taste, you could add 4 or 5 fillets, roughly chopped. Fresh bocconcini cheese (4 ounces [113 g]), sliced in half, ½ cup (50 g) of Pepe

Arrostiti (page 22) or some sliced avocado or radishes are also tasty additions. Or, you could make a winter panzanella filled with roasted root vegetables such as carrots, parsnips and butternut squash seasoned with rosemary or thyme and olive oil.

→ **Makes 8 to 10 servings** ←

Ingredients

8 oz (226 g) ciabatta or rustic sourdough, torn into bite-sized pieces

¼ cup (60 ml) extra virgin olive oil, divided

1 lb (454 g) ripe plum tomatoes, cut into quarters

1 small cucumber, peeled and sliced

½ red onion, finely chopped

¼ cup (60 ml) red wine vinegar

Salt and pepper, to season

A handful of fresh basil leaves, torn

Method

I like to toast the torn pieces of bread first. Preheat the oven to 350°F (175°C). Evenly coat the torn pieces of bread with some olive oil and place them onto a baking sheet. Toast for 10 to 15 minutes, or until golden brown. Put them into a large bowl to cool completely, and set aside.

Add the tomatoes, cucumber and red onion to the bowl. Add your choice of vegetables or cheeses to the salad. Extra virgin olive oil and red wine vinegar are essential in a panzanella, so add the remainder of the olive oil and the vinegar, adjusting them to your taste. I like a generous amount of olive oil, but you may enjoy more vinegar in your salad. Season well with salt and pepper and give the salad a toss to combine all the ingredients.

I love to present my panzanella on a large platter. Add the torn basil leaves, or other herbs, just prior to serving. Serve alongside my Slow-Roasted Lamb Shoulder (page 88).

Roasted Mediterranean Vegetables

Roasted seasonal vegetables are a fantastic way to complement any main dish—and they stand out on their own. This one-tray bake is all about adding fresh ingredients to one pan and allowing the flavors to combine. The best part about this dish is that you can use what you already have in your refrigerator.

Cooking doesn't need to be a tedious task; find ways to have fun with what you're creating. I love being super creative and experimenting with different flavors in the kitchen. Mediterranean cooking, especially vegetable dishes like this one, offers a variety of choices: eggplant, tomatoes, potatoes, peppers, zucchini and carrots, not to mention an array of herbs and spices.

Some vegetables cook quicker than others, so be mindful when pairing certain ingredients together. Harder vegetables, such as potatoes, carrots and sweet potatoes, will take a little more time than tomatoes, eggplant, summer squash and zucchini. The trick to perfectly cooked vegetables is to cut them into similar sizes. Cook the harder vegetables first, then add the peppers and tomatoes after 20 to 25 minutes, or halfway through the cooking process.

You also want to make sure that all the vegetables are seasoned well before they go into the oven, turning them occasionally throughout the cooking process. Your choice of herbs can help to elevate your roasted veggies; play around with some sage, oregano or bay leaf. These herbs have a slightly peppery flavor and work well with the vegetables. Go one step further and experiment with spices you have right in your kitchen. Use 1 teaspoon of ground cumin or paprika for a different flavor twist. These spices have a similar earthy taste, so one or the other would be a great addition. If you want a little citrus, sumac has a mild fruity taste that works perfectly with this dish, or add some freshly grated lemon zest.

Ingredients

1⅔ cups (250 g) cherry tomatoes

1 medium zucchini, cut into large pieces

1 red onion, peeled and cut into quarters

1 red pepper, seeded and cut into large pieces

6 cloves garlic, whole with skins

Extra virgin olive oil, to taste

1–2 tbsp (2–4 g) fresh rosemary or thyme leaves

Salt and freshly ground black pepper

Method

Preheat the oven to 350°F (175°C). Make sure to cut the vegetables into equal sizes. If you are adding some hard vegetables to the mix (potatoes, carrots, sweet potatoes or butternut squash), season them with a little olive oil, salt and pepper and your choice of herbs or spices, and put them into the oven 20 minutes before adding the remaining vegetables.

Place the tomatoes, zucchini, onion, pepper and garlic onto a large baking sheet. Drizzle them with a generous amount of olive oil and season with fresh rosemary or thyme leaves, along with your choice of additional herbs, and salt and pepper.

Give them a good mix and make sure all the vegetables are well coated with oil. Put them in the oven to roast for about 30 to 35 minutes, stirring them on occasion to prevent them from sticking to the baking sheet. Once cooked, the vegetables should be soft and slightly caramelized.

Serve on a large platter, drizzling the juices from the baking sheet over the vegetables.

Involtini di Melanzane

Eggplant is used in many recipes all over Italy, particularly in the southern regions. This is a satisfying vegetarian meal that can be assembled ahead of time. Involtini are very similar to rollatini. Rollatini are coated in bread crumbs and fried, and involtini are grilled then filled with ricotta. Serve involtini alongside my Baked Chicken Drumsticks (page 108) or beef meatballs (page 94) for an easy weeknight dinner.

Involtini ("small bundles") means to wrap around a filling, so I like to think of them as little parcels of deliciousness. They are super easy to make and take hardly any time at all to assemble. Often filled with a creamy cheese flavored with Parmesan and herbs, they are covered in tomato sauce, topped with mozzarella and baked in the oven.

Alternatively, thinly sliced zucchini or whole roasted peppers may be used as the base of the involtini, so if you have any in the refrigerator feel free to change it up and use one of these. Use 3 large zucchini, sliced into ¼-inch (6-mm) pieces or 4 whole red or orange bell peppers, cored and seeded. I suggest grilling the eggplant or vegetables of your choice until slightly charred for a little extra flavor and to help soften the vegetable, so it is easier to work with. You can dip the eggplant, zucchini or peppers in a little beaten egg, coat with some bread crumbs and fry them for extra crunch.

The filling can be changed and adapted to suit your taste. I've used ricotta, but you could use 8 ounces (226 g) of feta with some freshly grated lemon zest and fresh mint. Roughly chop 3 or 4 anchovies or 2 tablespoons (30 g) of capers for a savory kick.

If you have any of my Mum's Homemade Sugo di Pomodoro (page 14) in the freezer, use it. You can also use 2 to 3 cups (480 to 720 ml) of tomato puree or two 14-ounce (400-g) cans of diced tomatoes. If you love spicy food like I do, add 1 to 2 teaspoons (2 to 4 g) of dried red pepper flakes to the sauce for some extra heat.

Ingredients

2 lb (1 kg) eggplant (about 2 medium), cut lengthwise into ¼-inch (6-mm)-thick slices

Salt and freshly ground black pepper

Extra virgin olive oil, for brushing

8 oz (226 g) smooth ricotta cheese

1 egg

A handful of fresh parsley, finely chopped

Zest of 1 lemon

1 cup (100 g) grated Parmesan cheese, divided

2–3 cups (480–720 ml) Mum's Homemade Sugo di Pomodoro, divided (page 14)

8 oz (226 g) fresh mozzarella ball, roughly torn

Method

Arrange the eggplant slices in a colander. Sprinkle them with a little salt and allow them to sit for 30 minutes to draw out some of the moisture. It is okay if they overlap, just make sure they are evenly covered in the salt. Use a paper towel to gently wipe away any of the excess moisture from the eggplant, but please note that you can eliminate this step if you are using zucchini or red peppers.

Brush a little olive oil on each side of the eggplant slices and place some onto a hot grill pan. Grill on each side for 2 to 3 minutes, or until slightly charred. Transfer them to a plate and repeat with the remaining slices. Set them aside to cool completely. Repeat the same method with the bell peppers or zucchini if you are using them. You want them charred slightly and soft enough to shape.

Preheat the oven to 350°F (175°C). To make the filling, in a small bowl, mix together the ricotta, egg, parsley, lemon zest and ½ cup (50 g) of the Parmesan. Season well with salt and pepper and any other additions, such as anchovies or capers. Give the mixture a good stir. Prepare a large baking dish and pour 1½ cups (360 ml) of Mum's Homemade Sugo di Pomodoro (page 14) into the dish.

To assemble the involtini: Place 1 tablespoon (16 g) of the filling on one end of an eggplant slice. Use your hands to gently roll up and enclose. Put each involtini side by side into the baking dish, making sure they are packed tightly. Pour the remaining sauce over the involtini and scatter the torn mozzarella over the top of it. Sprinkle the remaining ½ cup (50 g) of Parmesan over top, reserving a little for garnish if you'd like. You could even nestle some torn basil in between the involtini, if you'd like.

Bake for 15 to 20 minutes, until the mozzarella and Parmesan have melted and are golden brown. Sprinkle more freshly grated Parmesan on top when serving if you wish. Serve with my Baked Chicken Drumsticks (page 108) or beef meatballs (page 94) for an easy weeknight dinner.

Pomodori Ripieni

Pomodori ripieni ("stuffed tomatoes") are a perfect starter or entrée for lunch or dinner and super simple to make. A feast for the eyes as well as the belly, this baked tomato dish originated in Rome and is filled with cheesy rice and herbs.

Though pomodori ripieni are commonly filled with rice, many Italian cooks add ground beef. It is a dish that can be made ahead of time. As mentioned, Italian cooking involves using all the ingredients on hand, so in this dish, the entire tomato is used, including the seeds, which are added into the simmering rice. Arborio rice can be quite heavy and starchy, so feel free to substitute basmati or long grain. For a lighter alternative, use an equal amount of dried quinoa or couscous. Please be mindful of the cooking times for the type of grain you use in this recipe, as they vary.

This recipe is for a vegetarian version, although many do add a protein (as mentioned above) for a heartier meal. You can keep it relatively simple with the ingredients listed or build on it. Use ½ pound (226 g) of ground beef or lamb seasoned with 1 to 2 teaspoons (2 to 4 g) of oregano, sage, basil or parsley. You can also include sausages in the filling mixed with 1 to 2 teaspoons (2 to 4 g) of fennel seeds.

Bell peppers can be substituted for the tomatoes. Since there is no inner flesh or juice from the pepper, add 1 (14-ounce [400-g]) can of chopped tomatoes when cooking the rice. Cut the tops off the peppers and carefully remove and discard the seeds and membranes.

I used ricotta salata, which is a firm cheese that has a similar consistency to feta, although it's not as salty. Shredded mozzarella, Parmesan, pecorino or feta are fine substitutes.

I love to add a layer of potatoes to the bottom of the pan, laying the tomatoes over the top. The combination of the roasted potatoes and stuffed tomatoes is out of this world!

→ Makes 10 stuffed tomatoes ←

Ingredients

10 medium, round, ripe tomatoes

2 tbsp (30 ml) extra virgin olive oil, plus more for drizzling

1 clove garlic, finely chopped

½ white onion, diced

2 tbsp (30 g) butter

1 tbsp (16 g) tomato paste

¾ cup (170 g) uncooked arborio rice

2 tsp (2 g) oregano leaves, fresh or dried

Salt and freshly ground black pepper

½ cup (120 ml) vegetable stock

1 cup (250 g) grated ricotta salata

½ cup (30 g) fresh parsley, finely chopped

4 medium-sized potatoes, cut into quarters

Method

Preheat the oven to 350°F (175°C). Prepare the tomatoes by first rinsing them and slicing off the tops. Keep the tops, as you'll put them back on the tomatoes before baking. Carefully scoop out and reserve the flesh, juice and seeds with a small spoon, trying not to damage the outer shell of the tomato. Place the hollow tomatoes into a baking dish.

In a medium saucepan over low-to-medium heat, warm the olive oil. Add the garlic, onion and butter, and cook for 2 to 3 minutes until the onion is soft and translucent. Stir in the tomato paste and cook for 2 to 3 minutes. Add the reserved tomato flesh, juice and seeds to the saucepan along with the rice and stir.

Season well with oregano or your choice of herbs, salt and pepper. I have added ½ cup (120 ml) of vegetable stock in this recipe because the amount of juice from the tomatoes will vary. Judge accordingly, as you may find that the amount of liquid from the tomatoes is enough to cook the rice. Add the vegetable stock as needed to achieve the desired consistency for the rice. Reduce the heat to low, cover and simmer for 20 to 25 minutes, until the rice has absorbed all the liquid. Set aside to cool for 10 minutes. The rice will continue cooking in the oven.

Stir the ricotta salata and fresh parsley into the rice. You can also use shredded mozzarella instead of the ricotta salata. Carefully fill each of the hollow tomatoes with a few tablespoons (about 30 g) of the rice mixture, filling them up just to the top. This filling will vary depending on the sizes of your tomatoes. Place them into a 9 x 9–inch (23 x 23–cm) baking dish. You can also grate a little more ricotta salata over the top, if you wish. Replace the tops of the tomatoes.

If you're adding some roasted potatoes to your dish, give them a head start in the oven as they will take a little longer to cook. Cut the potatoes and place them in the baking dish. Coat them with a little olive oil and season with a little salt and pepper. Remove them from the oven after about 30 minutes of cooking and add the tomatoes on top of the potatoes. Drizzle with a little olive oil, season with salt and pepper, place it into the oven and bake for 35 to 40 minutes, until the cheese has melted, the tomatoes are tender, the rice filling is cooked through and the potatoes are soft and golden.

Buttery Parmesan–Roasted Potatoes

Everyone loves crispy golden potatoes and, more often than not, there will be a potato dish served with an Italian lunch or dinner. When I was a child, my nonna would make her hand-cut potato chips by slicing the potatoes into disks and frying them in a little olive oil and generously salting them. My brother and I would eat them all the time as an afternoon snack. My grandmother even adds sliced potatoes to her frittata, which vanishes in less than 5 minutes after it hits the table. She definitely has a creative way of using potatoes, but I love them the traditional way: roasted with garlic and olive oil.

It is important to give these potatoes the right amount of preparation and seasoning. For really crispy roasted potatoes, it's essential to parboil them prior to roasting, as it allows the inside to become extra soft, creating a really crispy outer edge when baked. I boil them for about 6 to 8 minutes, in enough salted water to completely submerge them. Once drained, I pop them back into the pot, cover and shake vigorously to roughen them up.

Once they are seasoned, lay them flat onto a baking dish with enough room in between each potato. I find keeping them too close together will cause them to steam, which is definitely not what you're after. Give them enough space to allow the heat to travel evenly around them; use two baking dishes, if needed. Duck fat is amazing for getting that crispy outer edge. As this is not something that most people commonly have in their refrigerator, butter and olive oil can produce the same result. Try heating duck fat, butter or olive oil in the bottom of the baking dish before carefully adding the potatoes. This method will heat up the oil and give the potatoes a head start, contributing to that perfectly crispy outer edge.

Yukon Gold and russet potatoes are the best choices for roasting, but I use what I have on hand, as any potato is delicious! I like to keep the skin on the potatoes, but you can peel them if you prefer. Cut them so the pieces are all relatively the same size, about 1 to 1½ inches (2.5 to 4 cm). This is to ensure that they cook evenly. Of course, herbs play a big part in the taste of the dish. I have added fresh rosemary leaves to this dish, but you can shake it up a little with different kinds of herbs. When I say "a handful," I mean a decent amount, so use fresh herbs at your discretion. Alternatively, try dried herbs such as 1 tablespoon (about 3 g) of thyme, lemon thyme, sage, oregano or mix two together for a big punch of flavor.

Ingredients

2 lb (1 kg) baby potatoes, skin on

6 cloves garlic, whole and unpeeled

A handful of fresh rosemary, stems removed and leaves roughly chopped

2 tbsp (30 g) butter, melted

3 cloves garlic, minced

½ cup (50 g) grated Parmesan cheese

¼ cup (60 ml) extra virgin olive oil

Salt

Method

Preheat the oven to 350°F (175°C). Put the potatoes in a large pot of salted water and bring to a boil. Cook the potatoes for 6 to 8 minutes, until slightly soft. They will be ready when you can pierce them with a fork; they should be tender but not fully cooked, as they will continue cooking in the oven. Drain well in a colander, put them back into the pot and shake vigorously. This technique roughens them up to create a crispy texture when roasted.

Add the potatoes to a 13 x 9–inch (33 x 23–cm) baking dish, and leave enough room between them. If you feel they are too close together, evenly spread them out into two baking dishes. Sprinkle the garlic cloves and rosemary, or your choice of herbs, evenly all over the potatoes. In a small bowl, mix the melted butter and minced garlic together and pour generously over the potatoes.

Sprinkle the Parmesan over the potatoes. The butter will help it stick to the potatoes. Another hard cheese such as pecorino Romano works just as well. The added saltiness from the pecorino mixed with the garlicky potatoes is a dream.

Drizzle the olive oil over the top, season with salt and give it a generous toss, making sure all the ingredients are combined. Bake the potatoes for 35 to 40 minutes. Remove them from the oven after 20 to 25 minutes, gently turn each potato, and bake for another 15 to 20 minutes, until golden and crispy.

Serve the Buttery Parmesan-Roasted Potatoes alongside my Panzanella (page 132) and Slow-Roasted Lamb Shoulder (page 88).

Risotto alla Milanese

Risotto alla Milanese is an iconic and extremely hearty dish that comes from Milan in northern Italy. Making risotto is unlike cooking any other rice dish. It's cooked very slowly, adding ⅓ cup (80 ml) of broth at a time to allow the rice to release its starches slowly, creating a rich and creamy consistency. It is a delicate dish that requires time and patience.

Risotto can be made in many ways with some delightful flavor combinations. Mushrooms are a hearty addition to risotto. Sauté 1 pound (454 g) of mixed sliced mushrooms and a sliced leek until browned and mix them into the risotto with some fresh thyme leaves before serving. Another variation: Five minutes before the risotto is done cooking, add 1 pound (454 g) of cooked spicy Italian sausages with 10.5 ounces (84 g) of roughly chopped, sautéed kale. You could make it very cheesy by combining two of your favorite cheeses—Taleggio, fontina, Gruyère and mozzarella all work well in risotto. I suggest about 1 cup (112 g) total for the cheese, but if you're a cheese fan like me, feel free to add more.

This classic from the Lombardy region is not a dish to be tampered with, as it has very specific key flavors, although you can make a few slight alterations. Saffron threads are a vital ingredient in Risotto alla Milanese. Apart from the gorgeous golden color it produces in food, saffron provides a sweet, floral aroma and has a very unique taste. If you haven't had much experience with this spice, I recommend introducing it in small amounts, starting with about ½ teaspoon.

Turmeric powder, which has the same bright color as saffron, is a recommended substitute. Just be mindful when using this spice. It's not as sweet or floral as saffron, and it has a bolder, more peppery flavor. I suggest using about ⅓ teaspoon to start with.

Instead of chicken stock, you could add beef stock or a combination of 2 cups (475 ml) each of beef and chicken stock. Adding 2 ounces (50 g) of roasted beef bone

marrow or a fatty pancetta when you melt the butter will provide plenty of flavor, although it's not a necessity. Heat your oven to 400°F (200°C), put the marrow bones on a parchment-lined baking sheet, season with a little salt and bake for 20 to 25 minutes, until golden. Scoop out the marrow from the bones and add it to the risotto in the last 5 minutes of cooking.

It is no secret that risottos love cheese, Parmesan in particular. Pecorino Romano is another alternative. The trick to great risotto is allowing enough time for the grains to absorb the stock in its entirety, while making sure the rice is soft yet still has some bite. Once you master the art of making a creamy risotto, you'll be making it all the time.

Ingredients

4 cups (1 L) chicken stock

1 tsp saffron threads

2 tbsp (30 ml) extra virgin olive oil

1 shallot, finely diced

¼ cup (50 g) unsalted butter, divided

1½ cups (190 g) arborio rice

½ cup (120 ml) dry white wine

¾ cup (75 g) grated Parmesan or pecorino cheese

Method

Pour the chicken stock (or another stock of your choice) into a large pot over medium heat and bring to a gentle boil. Reduce the heat to low and simmer. Remove 1 cup (240 ml) of warm stock and add the saffron threads to it. Doing this helps to release the saffron's bright color, and when you add it to the rice, the yellow hue will be distributed evenly. If you are using turmeric as an alternative, set 1 cup (240 ml) of stock aside, add the spice into it and stir it well.

In a large saucepan over low heat, add the olive oil and shallot and sauté for 1 to 2 minutes, until it's soft and translucent. You may add bone marrow and 2 tablespoons (25 g) of the butter to the saucepan, or add this at the end, if desired.

Pour the arborio rice into the saucepan, stirring constantly to prevent the rice from sticking to the bottom. The grains should look slightly glassy. Increase to a higher heat and add the wine, stir and let it evaporate, about 1 to 2 minutes. Reduce the heat to low and add ½ cup (120 ml) of the heated stock and cook for 5 minutes, stirring continually, until the liquid has absorbed. Add ½ cup (120 ml) of stock every 5 minutes, including the saffron-infused stock, until all the stock has been used, about 35 minutes in total.

Add the Parmesan and remaining butter to the risotto, stirring until smooth and creamy. Cover with a lid and allow it to sit for 5 minutes prior to serving. This is to allow all the flavors to combine together. Serve with extra grated Parmesan, if desired.

Chapter Seven

The Sweet Escape

When thinking of Italian desserts, gelato, cannoli and, of course, tiramisu come immediately to mind. These classics are part of the history of Italian food culture, and over the years they have been showcased with their own unique flare. Pastries such as sfogliatella, which is a perfect on-the-go breakfast, or brioche con granita are eaten all over the country.

My family is from Basilicata in southern Italy, and we pride ourselves on traditional sweet treats that have been passed down from generation to generation. We typically make sweet treats during the holiday seasons of Christmas and Easter. Desserts such as crostoli, which are ribbons of fried dough coated in confectioners' sugar, are popular in our family. We also make scarpeddi, which is very popular in our region. It has a texture that is similar to a donut which is fried, covered in white sugar and eaten warm. It is ridiculously hard to stop at just one.

The recipes in this chapter are some of the foundational classics Italian dessert culture has been built on, and they are also extremely adaptable. For instance, my Tangy Lemon Granita (page 152) can easily be switched up with strawberries and fresh mint. The jam for the Sweet Peach Jam Crostata (page 156) can be replaced with frozen mixed berries. Do you have some leftover sponge cake? Make my Decadent Tiramisu (page 154) with a sponge base. When it comes to making desserts, the possibilities are endless.

Vanilla Bean Panna Cotta

A traditional dessert from Piedmont, in northern Italy, panna cotta is now found all over the country as well as the world. The smooth and creamy texture makes it the perfect dessert.

Panna cotta translates to "cooked cream" and has been adapted over the years. It is predominantly made up of gelatin, heavy cream, milk and sugar. The texture of panna cotta should be velvety smooth and light, and your spoon should glide straight through it like a knife. I'll admit it does take a little practice to get the hang of making panna cotta, but once you do, you'll be making it all the time, with lots of different toppings and flavor variations.

Heavy cream is quite rich in taste, so if you want something a little less intense, try using 2¾ cups (660 ml) of whole milk. Another great alternative is almond or oat milk using the same quantity.

You can also create other flavors. While you're heating the cream or milk, try infusing it with the zest from 1 orange or lemon, 1 heaping tablespoon (12 g) of finely ground coffee or 2 cinnamon sticks. Replacing the sugar with honey will create a deeper flavor.

This dessert is served with fresh mixed berries, but this is not a hard-and-fast rule. Depending on how you flavor your panna cotta, you could make a coffee syrup, a sweet compote, or perhaps add a little crunch with a hazelnut praline. No matter how you serve it, it is the perfect way to end a meal.

Makes 8 servings

Berry Compote

3 cups (480 g) fresh or frozen mixed berries

1 tsp granulated sugar

2 tbsp (30 ml) orange juice

Zest of 1 lemon

Panna Cotta

2½ cups (600 ml) heavy cream

⅓ cup (80 ml) whole milk

1 vanilla bean, split, or 1½ tsp (7 ml) vanilla extract

¼ cup (60 g) granulated sugar or honey

3 gelatin sheets

Method

To make the berry compote: Put the frozen or fresh mixed berries, sugar, orange juice and lemon zest in a medium saucepan and heat over low-to-medium heat. I love the combination of orange juice and lemon zest. You can most definitely use the whole orange, including the zest, in this recipe if you prefer. Stir well to combine all the ingredients. Once the fruit comes to a gentle boil, remove the pan from the heat and set aside to cool. This will allow the flavors to combine before you infuse the cream and milk. You can make the berry compote a day or two prior and keep it in an airtight container in the refrigerator until you are ready to serve the panna cotta.

To make the panna cotta: Heat the heavy cream, milk, vanilla bean and sugar in a saucepan over low heat and stir until the sugar is dissolved. You can adjust the amount of sugar or honey to suit your taste. The recipe calls for ¼ cup (60 g) of sugar, but you can reduce that by half. Flavor the cream with some cinnamon or the zest of a lemon or orange. It's important that you do not let the cream and milk come to a boil. As soon as you can see some steam coming off the mixture, take it off the heat. Then set it aside and allow it to cool slightly.

In a separate bowl, add the gelatin sheets one at a time in cold water so that it is submerged. Allow it to stand for 2 to 3 minutes, until it starts to soften. Add the softened gelatin sheets to the cream and whisk until completely dissolved. If the gelatin sheets have not completely dissolved, put the pan back over very low heat and whisk until smooth.

Prepare the panna cotta molds or glasses. It is important to strain the mixture through a fine-mesh sieve to remove any solids, then pour the strained liquid into individual molds or glasses. This helps to remove any little lumps that may not have melted. Divide the panna cotta mixture into the glasses or molds and put them into the refrigerator to set for a minimum of 4 hours or overnight. Be as creative as you want when presenting the panna cotta. Try a martini glass for a sophisticated look or on a small serving plate covered in berry compote. I present it in coffee glasses with the berry compote served on the top.

If you would prefer to remove the panna cotta from the molds, hold the molds under some hot water for about 5 seconds, and they should come out smoothly. Alternatively, insert a knife between the panna cotta and the mold to break the seal. Turn out onto a serving plate and shake gently to release. Serve with the berry compote.

Raspberry–Lemon Ricotta Cake

There is no doubt that Italians love ricotta. My take on this classic includes the heavenly complements of fresh raspberries and tart lemon zest. Ricotta cake is very common in Italy, and some Italians even eat a slice or two in the morning with their coffee.

This delectable cake is filled with fresh seasonal fruit to awaken the senses. It is soft, moist, buttery and tangy all at the same time. I love to use lemons in most of my cooking, and here they provide a beautiful fragrance as well as taste.

Raspberries work really well with the lemon, although blueberries, strawberries or mixed berries are the next best thing. One cup (about 150 g) of fresh or frozen berries is a good substitute. Frozen fruit tends to bleed a little when used in cakes and can darken the color. I recommend using fresh fruit when it's in season. You can remove the berries and use up those lemons you have lying around and make a lemon ricotta cake. Simply squeeze about 3 to 4 tablespoons (45 to 60 ml) or more of lemon juice into the cake batter.

If you love figs (like I do), slice 5 fresh ripe figs into quarters and layer them directly over the top of the cake with a generous drizzle of honey. The figs and the honey will caramelize in the oven and transform into a beautifully sticky sensation.

Almonds work wonders in this cake! Add 2 teaspoons (10 ml) of almond extract to the batter instead of the fruit. Scatter about ½ cup (54 g) of slivered almonds over the top of the cake before baking, and serve with a light dusting of confectioners' sugar.

Ingredients

1 cup (130 g) raw hazelnuts

2 cups (250 g) all-purpose flour

1 cup (200 g) granulated sugar

1½ tsp (7 g) baking powder

½ tsp salt

2 tbsp (6 g) espresso powder or instant coffee powder

3 large eggs

2 tbsp (30 g) butter, melted

1 tsp vanilla extract

Method

Preheat the oven to 375°F (190°C). Put the hazelnuts on a baking sheet lined with parchment paper and toast for 5 minutes or until golden. While they are still warm, use your hands or a tea towel to rub the skins off. You want to remove most of the skin, as it has a bitter taste, but if some still remain, that is perfectly fine. Once removed, coarsely chop the hazelnuts, or your choice of nuts, and set aside.

In a large bowl, sift the flour, sugar, baking powder, salt and espresso powder. In a separate bowl, add the eggs, butter and vanilla, and whisk to combine. Pour the egg mixture into the flour mixture and mix until combined. Add the nuts and fruit, if using, and mix until just combined.

Line a baking sheet with parchment paper. To prevent the dough from sticking to your hands, lightly cover them with a bit of water or oil. Put the dough onto a clean, lightly floured surface and shape into two 9-inch (23-cm)-long logs. Carefully place the logs onto the lined baking sheet and bake for 15 minutes, or until slightly golden on top. Remove the biscotti from the heat and allow them to cool for 10 minutes, long enough for you to be able to cut the logs into slices.

Carefully slice the logs diagonally into ¼-inch (6-mm) pieces and place them back onto the baking sheets, making sure you lay them flat. Pop them back into the oven and bake for another 15 minutes, until they are golden and firm. Once the biscotti are cool enough to handle, carefully transfer them to a wire rack to cool completely.

Serve the Coffee & Hazelnut Biscotti with a cup of espresso or a glass of vin santo.

Tangy Lemon Granita

Granita is a super-fluffy, icy dessert that is ideal during the warmer months. It is made up of granulated sugar and water, which creates a crunchy texture, then it's flavored with fresh seasonal fruit. In Sicily, granita is served with a fresh brioche bun for breakfast (a wonderful way to start the day) or as a snack in the summer.

The beauty of granita is the multitude of different flavors you can use. Replace the lemon used in this recipe with seasonal fruit such as watermelon, strawberries or pears. Coffee is used quite commonly in granita, which is a lovely way to start the day.

I use roughly 4 to 5 whole lemons in this recipe. If you are using fruit such as watermelon or strawberries, put 1 cup (140 g) into a blender and puree until nice and smooth. Taste and adjust the sweetness to your liking. Make sure to remove the skins and seeds of apples, pears or the like if you decide to use those. Sometimes I infuse the syrup with some lemon peel for some extra tartness.

Granita can also be made with fresh herbs for some extra flavor. I urge you to experiment with this. Lemon and fresh mint leaves work really well together—add 1 to 2 tablespoons (5 to 10 g) of chopped mint to the mixture just before freezing. Fresh thyme leaves will do the trick if you prefer more of a subtle taste.

Think of fresh herbs that will complement your choice of granita flavor. Basil works really well with watermelon; you could add a bunch to the blender and puree it together. For an adult twist, add a shot or two of your choice of flavored liquor, such as limoncello for a lemon granita or vodka for a watermelon and basil granita.

Be sure to use the freshest seasonal fruit you can find when making granita, although frozen fruit is fine. Use roughly the same amount, about 1 cup (140 g), of your choice of frozen fruit. You can also increase the sweetness by adding a teaspoon of honey.

Ingredients

1¾ cups (420 ml) water

1 cup (200 g) granulated sugar

Juice of 4 or 5 large lemons

Peel of 1 lemon

Mint leaves, for garnish (optional)

Method

Pour the water in a large saucepan over low heat and add the sugar. Whisk gently for about 3 to 4 minutes, until all the sugar has dissolved. Remove from the heat and cool slightly.

Add the lemon juice and lemon peel to the saucepan, and stir until combined. Set the mixture aside to completely cool and allow the flavors of the lemon peel to infuse and intensify. The trick is to get only the lemon peel with none of the pith, which has a bitter taste and can ruin the taste of the granita. Alternatively, you can grate the zest of 1 lemon and add it straight into the syrup.

Allow it to sit for a while to marry all those flavors. If you are using an alternative fresh or frozen fruit such as strawberries or watermelon, puree it, along with any fresh herbs, before adding it to the warm syrup. Thaw out any frozen fruit for 15 to 20 minutes prior to blending.

Cool for 10 to 15 minutes then, using a sieve, pour the liquid over a bowl and remove the lemon peel. I like to do this regardless of what flavors I am using, as it ensures a smooth consistency. Pour the liquid into a loaf pan, cover with a lid or a few layers of plastic wrap and put it into the freezer. If you don't have a loaf pan, any container with a lid will work just as well. Every half hour, remove the granita from the freezer and stir it with a fork to help break up the ice crystals. Repeat this method, every half an hour until it has completely set.

Remove the granita from the freezer 10 minutes prior to serving. Score the granita with a fork and scoop it into serving glasses. Serve it with freshly grated lemon zest or chopped mint leaves, if desired.

Decadent Tiramisu

Classic tiramisu is a rich Italian dessert made with light, creamy mascarpone cheese and layered Savoiardi ladyfingers soaked in coffee. It doesn't get any sweeter than that! There are so many different takes on tiramisu, but the basic ingredients do not vary. It's my favorite dessert!

It is not known where tiramisu originated. Some suggest it was created in Treviso in the 1800s, and over the years it has been adapted to suit individual tastes all around Italy. Original ingredients include the Italian Savoiardi ladyfinger, eggs, sugar, mascarpone cheese, coffee, cocoa powder and a flavored liqueur of some kind. Over the years the recipe has been adapted with cream to replace the eggs, as some people are uncomfortable using raw eggs. If this is the case, use 1¼ cups (300 ml) of heavy cream instead of the eggs.

Savoiardi ladyfingers are relatively easy to find in supermarkets, although you can actually use a loaf of pound cake instead. Cut it into ½-inch (1.3-cm)-thick slices, and follow the same method of soaking them in the coffee. Keep in mind that pound cake is not as dry as the Savoiardi, so you will need to work quickly so they don't break once they're dipped in the coffee.

When I went to parties as a little girl, there would always be a table with a complete spread of delicious desserts. There were two tiramisu dishes, one for the adults, which had the flavored liqueur, and the other for the kids, which was filled with chocolate. Chocolate milk was used instead of coffee, so we kids never missed out! If you don't want to add a flavored liqueur, such as Frangelico or Marsala wine to the dish, you can leave it out.

Ingredients

1½ cups (355 ml) freshly brewed hot espresso

1 shot (44 ml) Frangelico liqueur or Marsala wine (optional)

1¼ cups (300 g) mascarpone cheese

1 tsp vanilla extract or vanilla bean, halved and seeded

4 fresh eggs, separated, with yolks in one bowl and whites in another, divided

½ cup (100 g) granulated sugar

17.6 oz (500 g) package Savoiardi ladyfingers, or 1 lb (454 g) loaf cake, cut into ½-inch (1.3-cm)-thick slices

Cocoa powder, for dusting

Method

Pour the brewed espresso into a shallow bowl wide enough to accommodate the length of the Savoiardi ladyfingers. Add the flavored liqueur of your choice, if using, to the coffee and give it a little stir to combine. You can also use amaretto or brandy for a twist.

In another bowl, add the mascarpone and vanilla and use an electric mixer to beat gently until just combined, then set aside.

To the bowl of egg yolks, add the granulated sugar and, using the electric mixer, beat for 5 to 7 minutes until the yolks become thick and pale yellow. Set aside.

Clean the whisk attachments and dry them thoroughly. Beat the egg whites for 5 minutes, or until they form stiff peaks. Gently fold the egg whites into the beaten egg yolk mixture a little at a time until just combined. You want to make sure that you keep the mixture light and fluffy.

Gently fold in your mascarpone mixture into the beaten egg mixture, making sure it is well combined. If you are substituting cream for the eggs in this recipe, beat 1 cup (240 ml) for 2 to 3 minutes, until stiff peaks form, then gently fold it into the mascarpone mix.

Be creative in how you present the tiramisu to your guests—either as a showstopping centerpiece in a large ceramic dish or in individual glasses. Put a thin layer of mascarpone mixture on the bottom of the dish/glass to help keep the ladyfingers in place. Take one Savoiardi ladyfinger at a time and dip it into the coffee for just 1 or 2 seconds. You want to make sure that it is completely submerged in coffee, but take it out quickly, before it begins to fall apart. Create a layer of coffee-soaked ladyfingers, one at a time, on top of the mascarpone, until the base is completely covered. You may need to cut the ladyfingers in half, if you are using individual glasses or jars.

Carefully cover the ladyfingers with one-third of the mascarpone mixture and use a spatula to spread it out evenly. Repeat the process twice, layering the ladyfingers and finishing with the mascarpone mixture on top. Cover it with plastic wrap and refrigerate for at least 2 hours or overnight. I like to make mine the day before serving it, which allows all the flavors to develop.

Dust with cocoa powder just prior to serving.

Sweet Peach Jam Crostata

Crostata is a perfect ending to an Italian feast. This sweet treat is also a lovely complement to your afternoon coffee. The classic tart has a buttery shortcrust pastry and is filled with a thick homemade jam.

Making jam is a labor of love that results in a very sweet ending. I've used homegrown peaches in this crostata, but I encourage you to think outside the box when making your jam. The type of fruit you select depends on what's in season, but if your choice of fruit is unavailable, feel free to use frozen mixed berries or frozen peaches instead.

If you aren't keen on using a sweet jam, a delightful alternative would be to make crostata di ricotta. For the filling, whisk together 2¼ cups (550 g) of ricotta, 3 eggs, ¾ cup (150 g) of sugar, 1 teaspoon of vanilla, ½ teaspoon of ground cinnamon and the zest of 1 orange. You can even add ¼ cup (20 g) of finely chopped candied orange peel, which works beautifully with the orange zest and ricotta.

Experiment with different-flavored jam combinations. While using store-bought jam is absolutely fine, homemade really hits the spot, so I urge you to give it a try. You never know, you may just create a new family favorite! The peach jam can be made a few days in advance and can be stored in glass jars until you're ready to use it.

Peach Jam

5 medium ripe peaches

2 cups (400 g) granulated sugar

1 tsp ground cinnamon

Zest and juice of 1 lemon

¼ tsp ground cloves

Shortcrust Pastry

2 cups (250 g) Tipo 00 plain flour, or all-purpose flour, plus more for dusting

2 tbsp (30 g) granulated sugar

Zest of 1 lemon

1 tsp salt

4 tbsp (60 g) cold butter, cut into cubes

1 egg yolk

1 whole egg

1 tsp vanilla extract

1 tbsp (15 ml) iced water (optional)

Method

To make the jam: Thoroughly wash the peaches, and leave the skin on. Cut them in half, remove the pits and then cut the peaches into large cubes. Put the peaches into a large pot with the sugar, cinnamon, lemon zest and juice and ground cloves. Over medium heat, bring the mixture to a boil, then reduce to low heat so the fruit is brought to a simmer. Stir the jam constantly and skim any residue from the top. Simmer for about 1 hour, until the jam has thickened. Remove from the heat and allow to cool completely before pouring into jars and adding to the base of the crostata.

To make the pastry: In a large bowl, add the flour, granulated sugar, lemon zest and salt, whisking to combine. Work in the butter with your fingers until the mixture resembles coarse crumbs. To save time, you can add the ingredients to a food processor and pulse until you achieve the same consistency. In a separate bowl, add the egg yolk, egg and vanilla and mix to combine. Pour the egg mixture into the dry ingredients and mix until well incorporated. Pour onto a clean workspace and knead until it forms a soft dough. Unlike pasta or pizza dough, you don't want to work the dough very much, knead until just combined. If the dough feels a little dry, add a few teaspoons (5 to 15 ml) of iced water to loosen it. Wrap the dough in plastic wrap and refrigerate for at least half an hour.

Preheat the oven to 350°F (175°C). After the dough has rested, lightly dust a clean surface with flour, reserve ¼ of the dough for the top, and use a rolling pin to roll out the larger piece of dough to cover the base of an 8-inch (20-cm) tart pan or pie dish. Carefully lay the pastry over the base of the dish, making sure you cover the bottom as well as the sides evenly and you leave a 1-inch (2.5-cm) overlap to tuck these in. Roll out the remaining dough and cut out strips for the top of the tart using a knife or a pasta cutter. Spread an even layer of the cooled jam on the base of the tart, then pour on the remaining jam, until all of it has been used up. Decorate the top by layering the dough strips in a crisscross pattern, then fold the pastry edges inward to secure the tart.

Put the crostata into the oven and bake for 40 to 45 minutes, or until it is golden brown. Remove from the oven and let it cool completely in the tart pan prior to slicing.

Acknowledgments

It feels very surreal to be writing this, but, first and foremost, I would like to thank my family. To my extremely supportive Mum: I have been very lucky to have you as my pillar of strength over the years, especially during the last few months. Thank you so much for all the love and support.

Nonna Rosa, who is my inspiration for this cookbook: I have been very lucky to have you share 85 years of authentic cooking talent with me. I am honored and proud to share your very special talent with the world.

Zia Emilia, I could not have done this without your help over the past year. Your knowledge of the culinary world is absolutely incredible, and I thank you for all the help and support.

Thank you to all my family who have helped, tasted and tested the endless amount of food I've made over the last year and for all the kind words of encouragement, support and love.

To my Delightful Cook community and everyone who has been there from the beginning: It started out as a little blog on Instagram and now we are here. I'm so grateful for all the constant love and support I have received from you all over the years. I have made some wonderful friendships and I am truly grateful I get to do this job every single day.

To my editor, Sarah, and publisher, Will, thank you for guiding me through one of the most amazing experiences of my life. I am very appreciative of your patience, time and support. To the whole team at Page Street Publishing, thank you for taking a chance on me and giving me the opportunity I have always dreamed of. I am forever grateful.

About the Author

Caroline De Luca is a self-taught food photographer and writer based in Melbourne, Australia. Her large family extends from the busy streets of Melbourne to the little quiet town of Paterno, Basilicata, in southern Italy. Authentic Italian flavors and techniques were embedded in her DNA and practiced from childhood, learning about customs and traditional methods.

Her love for living *la dolce vita* started at a young age, and she developed a passion for the Italian way of life. Watching and learning from her family, she discovered a love for her southern Italian traditions and truly authentic home cooking. From this foundation of simple cooking, she has developed her own cooking style while still paying homage to her culinary roots. Learning about authentic home cooking from her family in both Australia and Italy has taught her how to turn simple ingredients into spectacular Italian dishes.

After leaving her day job to start her own business with her food blog, The Delightful Cook, she has worked as an editor with the food community at the feedfeed, written articles for *Eat.Live.Escape* and *Figs & Feta* magazines and has created content for some well-known brands within the industry, including Barilla, Bonne Maman Australia, realestate.com.au, John West Foods, Bertolli Australia, Vitamix Australia and so many others. She loves sharing her food endeavors with her growing community all across her social channels.

When she is not in the kitchen, Caroline loves to read, write and focus on her passion for acting. Her dream is to go on a yearlong food journey around Italy, exploring and eating her way through each and every region, one delightful dish at a time.

Index